A WAY TO RECONCILE
THE WORLD

AIKIDO STORIES FROM EVERYDAY LIFE

Edited by Quentin Cooke

i

A Way to Reconcile the World

Cover photograph by Simon Damiral of Atelier Wish Ltd

Cover design by Hugh Purser

Summary - A collection of aikido stories from aikido practitioners around the world about the impact of their practice in everyday life.

ISBN 978-1-63173-408-3

Cooke the Books

Contents

気 気 気

A Way to Reconcile the World

Introduction

This book was the idea of Robert Frager Sensei, a pioneer of aikido in the United States.

I was delighted to meet with him on a trip to California in 2012 and during our time together he said, "Someone needs to start collecting aikido stories." I immediately knew it was something that I wanted to do, and so I committed to it then and there. To find these stories, I had to connect with many *aikidoka* around the world. Nearly all of them were very encouraging and a high proportion helped me in my search.

The result is this book of stories from people around the world whose aikido heritages and histories are many and various. The stories exemplify the fact that at the heart of aikido lie powerful truths, which can be found whatever your aikido heritage is. As my own teacher, Koretoshi Maruyama Sensei, who studied under O Sensei, Morihei Ueshiba, the founder of aikido for a good number of years, says,

"Every river has a name. However, these names disappear when they flow into the great ocean. Aikido has many styles, many names, but aikido is aikido."

It has been a privilege to gather these stories, to liaise with the storytellers, and now finally to put them together for you. They are inspirational to a greater or lesser degree. Some are funny, but many are deeply moving and serve as a marvellous demonstration of aikido's power to transform people's lives for the better. They illustrate what O Sensei said, which is that aikido is *'a way to reconcile the world.'* Hence the title of the book.

If ever there was a powerful advert for the benefits of aikido, then this book is it. But the story doesn't end there! Firstly, my search for aikido stories goes on. Perhaps, as a reader, you will be inspired to write your own story, or maybe you know someone who has a tale to tell, in which case, please tell him or her to write it down and send it in. This volume is just the first of many, I hope. It is worth noting that whilst some of the stories received were just about word perfect, in many cases we were happy to work hard with the storytellers to improve the writing, whilst leaving their voice loud and clear, for everyone to hear.

Profits from this book will be used to support the work of Aiki Extensions (AE - *www.aiki-extensions.org*). AE is an international peacebuilding group based in America that employs the principles of aikido to bring about positive global change. The projects that AE sponsors bring transformation to the lives of people in some very difficult places around the globe. With your support AE can grow this wonderful work and make a more significant difference in the world.

As you read the stories, you will find that there are variations in the spelling of words, depending on the contributor's country of origin. We decided that this was just one subtle way in which we could preserve the personal voice of each storyteller.

We include rank, where the author wishes us to do so, along with the name and club of each author, not as an indication of worth, but in order to demonstrate that the practice of aikido can effect transformation in the newest beginner as well as the most seasoned sensei.

There is a glossary at the back of the book, which provides definitions for many words that we did not think would be automatically familiar. These are highlighted in italics throughout the text.

The task of gathering and weaving these tales together would have been much more difficult without the help of many generous people. So, I would like to thank the following people:

> Merle McKinley without whom this odyssey would never have begun.

- Robert Frager for providing the idea.
- Julia Harris and Jane Lott for their help in editing the tales and acting as sounding boards throughout the project.
- Linda Holiday, who had put together a smaller version of this book some years ago, and who has allowed me to re-publish the best of those tales. She has been very generous in her support throughout the project.
- Riki Moss, (partner of the late Terry Dobson), who has given me permission to re-produce the archetypal story of the type we sought, originally told by Terry himself. Many of you will know 'The Tokyo

Train Story,' but if you don't, then you have a treat in store. The book would not have felt complete to me without it. In addition, I consulted her and she was happy for us to print the story from Jerry Green about Terry.

- I also owe much to all those people, too numerous to mention, who helped get the message out there.
- Most of all I offer a huge 'thank you' to the storytellers themselves, many of whom have chosen to reveal aspects of their lives that are incredibly personal.

If you study aikido, may these stories remind you of why you train so hard, and if you do not already practice, then perhaps the following will motivate you to do so.

Quentin Cooke
Director of Aiki Extensions
Chair of Aikido for Daily Life

気　気　気

Foreword

The stories in this book provide marvelous insight into the depth and richness of aikido. They highlight aikido's potential to enhance our lives off the mat as well as on.

As a martial discipline, aikido is relatively easy to define technically. Aikido includes a wide assortment of throws, joint locks, strikes and pins. But these are only the outer forms of aikido, not aikido itself. Many technical manuals have been published covering aikido techniques. The stories in this book illustrate the fruits of the inner discipline of aikido.

In the 1960s, I was privileged to study directly with the founder of aikido, O Sensei Morihei Ueshiba. On one occasion I was travelling with O Sensei to the main Omoto Shinto shrine in Tokyo. As I was sitting with O Sensei in the back of a taxi, I realized this was a wonderful opportunity to ask him a question. Here I was, sitting next to a great master, the kind of sage that seekers travel to the Himalayas to find. I felt that I shouldn't waste this priceless moment. Then I wondered what to ask. I knew O Sensei was not patient with people who asked foolish questions and I thought, "This had better be a good question."

I gathered up my courage and asked, "Sensei, what is the correct attitude to our training partners in aikido?" He smiled and I was relieved that he seemed to like my question. O Sensei replied, "It is like a parent to a child. You lead your training partners with the expectation that they will follow you." I have thought about his answer ever since. Good parents are loving and authoritative, and their directions are clear and easy to follow. Look closely at the videos of O Sensei and you will see the love and joy in his face as he demonstrated aikido. We were all his children. For me, he was the embodiment of aikido, and I'm still learning from his example.

O Sensei taught that the goal of aikido is to work toward world peace, to transform violence into harmony, to make an enemy into a friend. How does aikido accomplish this? Aikido training teaches us to become centered, to remain calm and balanced under pressure. Aikido teaches us to be acutely aware of our training partners and to perceive their intention to attack, which allows us to counter an attack before it begins. This awareness carries over to daily life.

Aikido teaches us to interact with our training partners with the intention of neutralizing their attacks, rather than seeking to defeat them. In the terms of conflict resolution, we learn to seek 'win-win' solutions rather than 'win-lose' solutions. Hours of training with this attitude carry over into our daily lives as well. And, ideally, aikido teaches us to interact with each other with love and joy.

In 1975, I founded Sofia University (formerly known as the Institute of Transpersonal Psychology). From the beginning, I required aikido training for all our residential psychology graduate students. Year after year, my students found their aikido training was as valuable as their psychology training.

I require my graduate students keep aikido journals, and every year I've read dozens of stories like the ones in this book. Aikido training has powerfully affected my students' relationships. It has helped them handle a wide variety of conflict situations gracefully. Perhaps the most dramatic examples I've read occur during school holidays when students return home and have to cope with their families. They have often been pleasantly surprised at their newfound abilities to remain calm and centered during challenging family interactions and to communicate effectively with those who had never really listened to them before.

How is aikido a martial art? For one thing, the techniques **do** work in real life. Aikido techniques are rooted in centuries-old, highly effective jiu jitsu practices. For another, the best martial art is the one that teaches you to avoid conflict whenever possible.

When I first started training, I was told a fascinating aikido story. My aikido colleague was working as a policeman when the story occurred. He had been a highly successful judo and karate competitor, and he had only six months of aikido training at that time.

One Friday evening, he pulled over a car filled with high school boys after the driver ran through a stop sign. The boys piled out of the car and surrounded him in a half circle. They were all husky young men. They looked like high school football players. As my colleague began writing out a ticket for the driver, he felt that the boy on his far left was getting ready to swing at him. He turned, looked the young man in the eye, and thus defused the impending attack. After the boys left, he sat in his patrol car reflecting on the incident. He somehow knew that his awareness came from his six months of aikido training, not from his years of judo and karate. (This experience eventually led him to become a full time aikido teacher.)

I can't tell you exactly how aikido is such an effective awareness and centering practice, but the stories in this book provide similar, real life examples of the value and benefits of aikido training. I hope that the more we all become aware of this dimension of aikido training, the better we can practice it, teach it, and live it.

Robert Frager Ph.D.
Sofia University Dojo - U.S.A.
President, Western Aikido Association (affiliated with the Aikikai
Foundation, Japan)
7th Dan

気　気　気

In the Beginning
by
Quentin Cooke - Burwell Aikido Club - England - 7th Dan

I often liken my study of aikido to an ongoing journey. I am not quite sure of my destination, I just know enough to keep putting one foot in front of the other. The thing about any journey is that even with the best of plans, one must be prepared for the occasional surprise.

Recently, it feels as if the fates have conspired to shape the path I travel in a very positive way. I will explain this by sharing the story of how this book came about. To me, it exemplifies what can happen if you just keep on going.

I live near Cambridge in England and see aikido very much as a philosophy for life. It provides us with important principles that I believe can genuinely transform the world. A tool that can neutralise a violent attack and produce a positive outcome is a powerful tool indeed.

I am simply trying to follow the steps of O Sensei himself, who described aikido as the "art of peace" and "a way to reconcile the world." These ideas form the core of my study, and as such, I strongly believe that we have to find a way of getting the message of aikido off the mat and into the society as a whole. This seems to be the way to go, because the odds look well and truly stacked against the possibility of persuading the world at large to step onto the mat and experience what we do when we train.

For this reason, I have been a big supporter of Aiki Extensions (AE) and I am, in fact, a board director. Its mission is to connect people of like minds and to use the tool of aikido to make a better world. The intention is to infuse principles learned on the mat into business, schools, government, therapy, local communities, and indeed to channel such goodwill toward any place where those involved could enjoy a more satisfying outcome.

In simple terms, we aim for the stars and it will come as no surprise to learn that more often than not, we fall short. On a personal level though, it has meant that I have met and become friends with some truly amazing people across the world that I would never have otherwise known. Their wisdom, generosity and general good heartedness has been inspirational. Nevertheless, we have a long way to go before AE is recognised as a significant movement within the aikido community as a whole, and that takes me to this particular tale.

Towards the end of 2011, AE ran a campaign to encourage new membership. We decided to offer raffle prizes for anyone who joined during the month in question. Each board member was asked to come up with something to give. I offered to teach three private lessons at my *dojo* as one prize and also to teach a course for free, which would include travel expenses, if it were local. Whilst the uptake was not huge, the raffle had some impact and a draw was held to see who won what. Now I will come back to the winner of the private lessons later in my tale, but suffice to say here, that the winner of the other prize was a lady in California called Merle McKinley.

I raised my eyes to the skies and thought, "Well that isn't going to go anywhere," but duly sent an email to her to advise her of her good fortune, if that is what it was. Frankly, I expected nothing more than a 'thank you', and thought that would be that. To my surprise, she emailed me back to say that she was delighted, as she had never won anything before and that she had no idea that when she joined that there was even the potential of winning a prize.

She went on to say that, in fact, she had thousands of air miles that were due to expire and had been thinking of possibly using them to come to England, but she now wondered if I might like to use them to go to California. I nearly fell off my chair! I told her that this was her prize and of course I could come, but if she preferred, she could come to my home and I could offer a series of private lessons. Merle decided that she would like me to come to California and then went on to tell me that what she really wanted to do was to use me as an excuse to visit many of the local high ranked teachers peppered around the San Francisco Bay Area.

There are probably more sixth and seventh *dan* teachers within a two hour radius of where I was going to be staying than anywhere else in the world. Many of them are names familiar to anyone who has been involved in aikido for a while. Now at this point, I truly began to wonder if I were dreaming. Needless to say, I told Merle that of course I would be happy to comply. I had to keep reminding her that this was her prize, even if it felt increasingly like mine. The good news was that through my host's local knowledge and my connections in AE and beyond, we were able to put together a trip that was to die for.

I trained with some outstanding people, most of whom were far more experienced than I. I got to teach in a number of their *dojos* and had one-to-one time with many of the teachers, either sharing a coffee or a meal. It was a life changing experience, in which I gained important training insights on the mat and also learnt about myself and what I have to offer.

I was amazed at how well my own teaching was received and how grateful people seemed to be that I was there. I kept thinking that I was the one who should feel grateful, and I most certainly was. I forged wonderful new connections and found inspiration and support for AE, which I talked about wherever I went. I came away with a clear idea of what we need to do to further AE's mission and have been working on that ever since. (*As stated in the introduction, one of the ideas, given to me by Robert Frager Sensei was the creation this book*).

As if the tale so far were not already unlikely enough, many small things occurred during the trip that seemed way beyond coincidence. For example, my host's house was in Cambridge Lane, (*remember where I live*).

At Aikido of Santa Cruz, I had lunch with Linda Holiday Sensei. We were joined by the lady who won the private lessons back in the UK. She had been a student of Linda's before she moved back to the UK and she just happened to be visiting at this time.

Finally, about two weeks before I was due to travel to the United States, I received an email from a gentleman there, who I did not know. Like me, he supported an initiative called Peace Dojos International. He wrote to me about a problem he was having with an individual who was claiming a patent on certain words that he was using in his own marketing material. I decided that whilst there was not much practical support I could give, I would at least acknowledge the communication and offer some moral support. This lead to an email exchange, in which he used me to gain feedback on an email that he planned on sending to the person in question. On this, I was able to offer some real help.

It was a natural consequence of our exchange to tell him that I was going to be visiting the States soon and to enquire as to where he lived. It turned out that he lived 35 minutes away from my host's house. Given that he could have hailed from anywhere within the vastness of the United States of America, this seemed incredible. We did connect during my visit and, in fact, our discussions were some of the most interesting that I held.

California is truly an amazing place. For the *aikidoka*, it is a pilgrimage to be made. The Californians are a different breed. They have a holistic view of humanity, which seems integral to their way of being. As a result, wherever I went, regardless of training style or lineage, I felt very at home.

So the point of all this is simply that you tend to reap what you sow. In my case, I had been banging the AE drum for a while and at times wondered if anyone was listening and whether there was any point. I was not expecting the crop that grew, but it was a direct result of what I had been doing. I gained hugely and it has changed me forever. Furthermore, I came away with many ideas that can help to further AE's mission, of which this book is one. (*Maybe if this tale has inspired you, you can be part of that by signing up to AE*).

Happy travelling and I do hope to share the journey with you at some point! Now please read on, as the following tales are truly inspirational. They are wonderful examples of how aikido can impact upon so many aspects of our lives and how it can be used to change our world for the better in incredible ways.

気　気　気

The Tokyo Train Story
by
Terry Dobson

A turning point came in my life one day on a train in the suburbs of Tokyo, in the middle of a drowsy spring afternoon. The old car clanked and rattled over the rails. It was comparatively empty; a few housewives with their kids in tow, some old folks out shopping, a couple of off-duty bartenders studying the racing form. I gazed absently at the drab houses and dusty hedgerows.

At one station the doors opened, and suddenly the quiet afternoon was shattered by a man bellowing at the top of his lungs, yelling violent, obscene, incomprehensible curses. Just as the doors closed, the man still yelling, staggered into our car. He was big, drunk and dirty. He wore labourer's clothing. His front was stiff with dried vomit. His eyes bugged out, a demonic, neon red. His hair was crusted with filth. Screaming, he swung at the first person he saw, a woman holding a baby. The blow glanced off her shoulder, sending her spinning into the laps of an elderly couple. It was a miracle that the baby was unharmed.

The couple jumped up and scrambled toward the other end of the car. They were terrified. The labourer aimed a kick at the retreating back of the old lady. "YOU OLD WHORE !" he bellowed, 'I'LL KICK YOUR ASS!" He missed, as she scuttled to safety. This so enraged the drunk that he grabbed the metal pole in the center of the car, and tried to wrench it out of its stanchion. I could see that one of his hands was cut and bleeding. The train lurched ahead, the passengers frozen with fear. I stood up.

I was young and in pretty good shape. I stood six feet, and weighed 225 lbs. I'd been putting in a solid eight hours of aikido training every day for the past three years. I liked to throw and grapple. I thought I was tough. Trouble was my martial skill was untested in actual combat. As students of aikido, we were not allowed to fight.

My teacher, the founder of aikido, taught us each morning that the art was devoted to peace. "Aikido," he said again and again, "is the art of reconciliation. Whoever has the mind to fight has broken his connection with the universe. If you try to dominate other people, you are already defeated. We study how to resolve conflict, not how to start it."

I listened to his words. I tried hard. I wanted to quit fighting. I even went so far as to cross the street a few times to avoid the *chimpira*, the pinball punks who lounged around the train stations. They'd have been happy to test my martial ability. My forbearance exalted me. I felt both tough and holy. In my heart of hearts, however, I was dying to be a hero. I wanted a chance, an absolutely legitimate opportunity whereby I might save the innocent by destroying the guilty.

"This is it!" I said to myself as I got to my feet. This slob, this animal, is drunk and mean and violent. People are in danger. If I don't do something fast, somebody will probably get hurt. I'm gonna take his ass to the cleaners."

Seeing me stand up, the drunk saw a chance to focus his rage. "AHA!" he roared, "A FOREIGNER! YOU NEED A LESSON IN JAPANESE MANNERS!" He punched the metal pole once to give weight to his words.

I held on lightly to the commuter-strap overhead. I gave him a slow look of disgust and dismissal. I gave him every bit of piss-ant nastiness I could summon up. I planned to take this turkey apart, but he had to be the one to move first. And I wanted him mad, because the madder he got the more certain my victory. I pursed my lips and blew him a sneering, insolent kiss. It hit him like a slap in the face.

"ALL RIGHT! he hollered, "YOU'RE GONNA GET A LESSON." He gathered himself for a rush at me. He'd never know what hit him.

A split-second before he moved, someone shouted "HEY!" It was ear splitting. I remember being hit by the strangely joyous, lilting quality of it, as though you and a friend had been searching diligently for something, and he had suddenly stumbled upon it. "HEY!"

I wheeled to my left, the drunk spun to his right. We both stared down at a little old Japanese. He must have been well into his seventies, this tiny gentleman, sitting there immaculate in his *kimono* and *hakama*. He took no notice of me, but beamed delightedly at the labourer, as though he had a most important, most welcome secret to share. "C'mere," the old man said in an easy vernacular, beckoning to the drunk, "C'mere and talk with me." He waved his hand lightly. The big man followed, as if on a string. He planted his feet belligerently in front of the old gentleman, and towered threateningly over him. "TALK TO YOU," he roared above the clacking wheels, "WHY THE HELL SHOULD I TALK TO YOU?" The drunk now had his back to me. If his elbows moved so much as a millimeter, I'd drop him in his socks.

The old man continued to beam at the labourer. There was not a trace of fear or resentment about him. "What'cha been drinking?" he asked lightly, his eyes sparkling with interest. "I BEEN DRINKING SAKE," the labourer bellowed back, "AND IT'S NONE OF YOUR GODDAM BUSINESS!" Flecks of spittle spattered the old man.

"Oh, that's wonderful," the old man said with delight, "absolutely wonderful! You see, I love sake too. Every night, me and my wife (she's 76, you know), we warm up a little bottle of sake and take it out into the garden, and we sit on the old wooden bench that my grandfather's first student made for him. We watch the sun go down, and we look to see how our persimmon tree is doing. My grandfather planted that tree, you know, and we worry about whether it will recover from those ice-storms we had last winter. Persimmons do not do well after ice-storms, although I must say that ours has done rather better than I expected, especially when you consider the poor quality of the soil. Still, it is most gratifying to watch when we take our sake and go out to enjoy the evening, even when it rains!" He looked up at the labourer, eyes twinkling, happy to share his delightful information.

As he struggled to follow the intricacies of the old man's conversation, the drunk's face began to soften. His fists slowly unclenched. "Yeah," he said slowly, "I love persimmons, too... His voice trailed off. "Yes", said the old man, smiling, "and I'm sure you have a wonderful wife."

"No," replied the labourer, "My wife died." He hung his head. Very gently, swaying with the motion of the train, the big man began to sob. "I don't got no wife, I don't got no home, I don't got no job, I don't got no money, I don't got nowhere to go. I'm so ashamed of myself." Tears rolled down his cheeks, a spasm of pure despair rippled through his body. Above the baggage rack a four-color ad trumpeted the virtues of suburban luxury living.

Now it was my turn. Standing there in my well-scrubbed youthful innocence, my 'make this world-safe-for- democracy' righteousness, I suddenly felt dirtier than he was.

Just then, the train arrived at my stop. The platform was packed, and the crowd surged into the car as soon the doors opened. Manoeuvring my way out, I heard the old man cluck sympathetically. "My, My," he said with undiminished delight, "that is a very difficult predicament, indeed. Sit down here and tell me about it."

I turned my head for one last look. The labourer was sprawled like a sack on the seat, his head in the old man's lap. The old man looked down at him with compassion and delight, one hand stroking the filthy, matted head.

As the train pulled away, I sat down on a bench. What I had wanted to do with muscle and meanness had been accomplished with a few kind words. I had seen aikido tried in combat, and the essence of it was love, as the founder had said. I would have to practice the art with an entirely different spirit. It would be a long time before I could speak about the resolution of conflict.

気　気　気

The Power of Story
by
Linda Holiday - Aikido of Santa Cruz - U.S.A. - 6th Dan

Storytelling must be as old as human language itself. Stories I've heard from my aikido teachers have inspired my practice for more than 40 years. When you hear a profound story, you feel in some way as if you have experienced it yourself. It becomes a part of you.

One of my teachers, Terry Dobson, was a vivid storyteller. When he taught at my *dojo* in Santa Cruz, California in the 1970s, my students and I would listen in rapt attention as he told stories about his experiences in Japan with O Sensei, the founder of aikido, and anecdotes of life on the aikido path in America. When some of Terry's stories were published a few years later, I would read them aloud in class so that these enlightening experiences would live in my newer students as well. One vivid story was published in a magazine in 1981 under a title that was, at that time in aikido history, a novel concept: "The Martial Art of Not Fighting." It told the tale of how Terry stopped an act of violence on the street, at a distance, through the use of *kiai*: a burst of concentrated energy that most often takes the form of a shout. It was a dramatic portrayal of the power of focused intention and the desire to protect life. Lessons that Terry had learned from O Sensei himself.

One clear afternoon in downtown Santa Cruz, as I was driving along Water Street in the direction of my *dojo*, the light turned red at the intersection and I brought my car to a stop. It was a large intersection by Santa Cruz standards, with double lanes of traffic in all directions plus left-turn lanes, sidewalks, and bike lanes. Alone in my car, I gazed at the surrounding area: a few bank buildings, a Mexican restaurant, several people walking toward the post office. A young man on a bicycle came to a stop on the cross street to my left, waiting for the light to change, alongside a large white car.

Suddenly the door on the driver's side of the car was thrown open, and a large man jumped out and ran around the back of the vehicle toward the bicyclist. The man's business suit contrasted oddly with his rapid and agitated movement. In a flash, he reached the young man, seized him by the shoulders, dragged him off the bike, and threw him roughly onto the cement. What previous interaction between them could have sparked this act of aggression, I could not imagine. But there was no mistaking the rage in the man's posture as he crouched over the younger man who he had slammed to the ground. It seemed that the aggressor had completely lost his self-control and was about to strike or choke his victim.

This harsh sight reached my body and mind like a shock wave. It happened so fast I had no time to think about it, but I experienced an immediate sense of "wrongness" and a visceral desire to make the violence stop. In my car, four lanes away, it seemed there was no way I could reach the scene in time to make a difference to the outcome.

Then, instinctively, my left hand cranked the handle that lowered the car window at my side, and through that opening the strongest *kiai* of my life shot out of me, aimed directly at the man poised violently over the cyclist.

"NO!" I shouted, "STOP THAT! YOU MUST STOP!" I felt a tremendous energy pouring through my voice. It was the longest-range *kiai* I had ever done, yet it felt just the same as the clear, focused shouts I had practiced and taught in aikido *dojos* for years. The sense of *ki*, connection, and the intention to protect life was unmistakable.

At that moment, the man in the suit abruptly looked up, released his double-handed grip on the bicyclist, and stood up as if he had suddenly awakened out of a violent dream. He walked back to his car, got into the driver's seat, closed the door, and drove away across the intersection. The young man picked himself up off the cement, climbed back onto his bicycle, and rode across the intersection, wobbling a bit. He threw one arm up in a defiant gesture toward the white car as it receded in the distance. The whole incident couldn't have taken more than a few minutes. The light in front of me turned green.

What I felt, as I drove on, was euphoria. Thanks to aikido training, an act of violence had been interrupted and stopped, from a safe distance, by *ki* and sound alone! The story I had heard from Terry Dobson so many years before was vividly present in my mind. Suddenly, the afternoon sunlight seemed especially brilliant. I felt newly connected to O Sensei's teaching of "the spirit of loving protection for all." I felt like singing!

As is often the case, one story leads to another. A few nights later, I recounted my experience to a class of students at my *dojo*, who were deeply captivated by the story. Then we all practiced projecting power and intention through *kiai*, using both the traditional, short Japanese sounds as well as words in English. Right after the class, one of the students, a slender young woman, was walking to her car when she saw two men engaged in a fistfight. A crowd had gathered to watch, but no one had intervened. Drawing upon the practice of *kiai*, my student projected her voice from a safe place in the darkness, and shouted, "STOP THE FIGHT! I'M CALLING THE POLICE!" To her amazement, the fight quickly came to a halt, and the crowd dispersed.

There is a powerful, life-protecting force in each of us that can be used for peace and healing. Stories help us know about that power, and give us the courage to use it.

Let's keep telling aikido stories.

気　気　気

Children in Transformation at the Bronx Peace Dojo
by
Bill Leicht - Bronx Peace Dojo - U.S.A. - 1st Dan

The Bronx Peace *Dojo* in 2003 was based at F.R.I.E.N.D.s, a family crisis center of the Visiting Nurse Association in the old South Bronx. Our participants were neighborhood children and the Center's own young clients. The children, seven to thirteen years old, all lived in this very disrupted area. Those who were clients were in treatment for serious emotional and behavioral disorders. I asked that counselors join their clients for classes, so that they could encourage them and learn more about their children in a group setting focused on physical and verbal peacemaking as play.

"Kevin" (a pseudonym) entered the Peace *Dojo* with his counselor and immediately lost his temper. He was the smallest and most agitated of the children and at seven, the youngest. Nonetheless, he began to play and to pay attention for short periods during lessons. He learned with the others about tummy breathing, sitting and relaxing as well as how to grasp the wrist of his partner, or to have the partner grasp his, in a simulated attack.

The other children taught Kevin about their Peace Place at the corner of the mat space. They also showed him how to notice when he was starting to get angry (breathing very fast, tightening shoulders). They themselves would go to the Peace Place when that happened, would take a brief time out, then when their breathing slowed, they felt relaxed, and no longer angry, they would get back on the mat.

Kevin started trying out their pattern, going to the Peace Place many times during a class when other children reminded him that he was getting upset. At first he would stay there for a few minutes. Within a mere two weeks he was, on his own initiative, using the Peace Place far less, staying only a few seconds, then coming back on the mat smiling. He also asserted his right as its primary user to rename the Peace Place the "Kool-out Corner."

His counselor said that although he had been in therapy for more than six months, his behavior had changed radically within the first two weeks of his Peace *Dojo* practice. We created a slide show, "The Bronx Peace *Dojo* in Action." Its photograph of Kevin in his Kool-out Corner being attended by another student was a highlight. It also demonstrated in the milieu of the Peace *Dojo*, that the students themselves unselfconsciously supported each other's growth and normal behavior. The Bronx Peace *Dojo* became very much their own.

気　気　気

From Movement to Magic
by
Aimee Bernstein - U.S.A.

At eighteen, a friend asked me who I envisioned myself to be at fifty. Without hesitation I responded, "A woman of character." That answer has directed and informed my life ever since. Though there have been many moments when I have wished to be a mother, a wife, a financially successful career woman, the only desire that has been steadfast and compelling has been to discover and live the truth of who I am. The path has not always been smooth and direct. I've chased the dollar and have been seduced by love more times than I choose to admit. Yet, I have never forgotten for very long what is most important to me. Always, I have known that true wealth comes not from the material but from a connection to what some call "The Source of All That Is." Others refer to this Higher Power as the Tao, Yahweh or God. All other relationships, be they with myself or others, are dependent on this primary connection. In fact everything in life is.

Many years later, I would read O Sensei's words… *"How can you straighten your warped mind, purify your heart, and be harmonized with the activities of all things in Nature? You should first make God's heart yours."* However, at eighteen, I knew nothing about aikido or even religion. Nevertheless, I intuited that there was something more within me that would shape my life for the better.

The challenge of my life has been learning to loosen the hold of my personality, which pinches from time to time in its containment of me. When my personality with all it desires, needs and preferences chatters too loud, Source becomes the echo of a distant note that I fail to hear. On the road to discovering my character, I've sometimes confused the voice of my personality with that of a higher consciousness. In those times, I've always come up a dollar short. Yet these experiences have taught me a great deal about aligning to Source. I'd like to tell you now about one of those times and what it taught me about true wealth.

In my mid-twenties, I began studying aikido. Though not much of an athlete, I had stepped onto the mat in the hopes of learning what my teacher, Robert Nadeau, knew about how the human system aligned to universal energies. I wanted to discover, not just intellectually but with every ounce of my being, my relationship to Source. I was looking for true wealth, although I didn't recognize it as such at the time. I chose to study with Nadeau because he provides the clearest and most comprehensive map to establish a connection with Source that I have found.

After training for a few years, I finally took my brown belt test. This was an auspicious occasion for me. In my mind, a brown belt rank marked the beginning of mastery. For months, I practiced diligently for my test with Sue Ann, the best of the aikido students. Eager to exemplify the *budo* spirit I admired, I forged forward despite sprained ligaments and sore knees. With her assistance, I came to know each technique intimately. My stance was strong and my determination to demonstrate excellence abundant. I knew that a great performance did not occur through technique alone. As Nadeau taught, it required an alignment with universal energies. This alignment allows inspiration to come through transforming simple movement into magic. I was ready for the magic, ready to join the ranks of the special few, whose tests were talked about for years to come. I wanted to make my teacher proud and to distinguish myself as one who really knows.

Confidently, I stepped onto the mat when my name was called. To my surprise, Sue Ann came forward with a fury I had not previously experienced. It took everything I had to successfully deal with her attack. At first, I felt angry; then I realized that what had appeared as confidence was really fear, so that I became so frozen in my body that I could hardly move. Sue Ann's powerful attacks were her way of trying to rouse me from my rigidity.

Her strategy worked and I was able to demonstrate each required technique. But was my test memorable? Hardly! Though people congratulated me afterwards, I felt a cold disappointment that reeked of failure. And when Nadeau, who usually made students wait a week to receive their certificates, hurried back to his office to write mine out, I felt ashamed and angry. Ashamed that I had not achieved the brilliant performance I had envisioned; angry that Nadeau could accept anything less from me.

Though I was not a drinker, I stopped on my way home that night and bought a bottle of whisky. Not knowing anything about whiskey I bought a bottle of Yukon Jack advertised as 'The black sheep of Canada.' Its name represented how I felt inside. Clearly I was young, distraught and overly dramatic.

I sat on my patio, taking slugs from my bottle while trying to come to terms with my perceived failure. "My test was quite average," I bemoaned. "Therefore, I must be average." I sat with this thought for a while allowing it to sink in. A couple of slugs later my pride took over and announced, "Well, not really average - maybe a little above average - but certainly not extraordinary." Both were voices of my personality trying to find truths they could not know. For a couple of hours they debated until they exhausted each other.

As the voices stilled, the brilliance of the starlight attracted my attention. I noticed the trails of light that led from one star to the other. What had appeared as separate entities were now linked in a mosaic that went further than my eye could see.

Everything was connected, yet, in my limited view, I could not perceive its grand design. At that moment, I realized I had been operating with a great misunderstanding. I had pursued a relationship with Source in order to become a better person, more highly functioning and more enlightened. And Source, being what It is, had allowed me to do so, offering me enough results to keep me interested. My search for character and spirituality, I realized was as ego driven as my search for money and love.
That night I learned not to cling too tightly to external results, to how I appear or how I compare in the world. I saw how in choosing image and ambition, I lost sight of who I am. I realized that what seemed like an average test was really quite a significant leap for me. It was more than my new ability to demonstrate techniques; the disciplined training had transformed me from the inside out. Though I did not recognize it immediately, Nadeau had.

That night I learned that what appears as greatness seems ordinary once you achieve it. From the new vista, an even higher plateau brimming with new energies and possibilities looms and calls. And so the Source of All That Is continuously reveals itself and the process of growth occurs. But what truly changed my life is that I made a new decision that night. Instead of using Source, I would allow Source to use me.

Thirty years later, each day has become an opportunity to choose to be of service to the Source of All That Is. Though at times I still resist, I notice the face in the mirror has more character these days. And though my banker still does not consider me a preferred customer, as my willingness to serve spirit deepens, I know that I have become a very wealthy woman.

(*First published in* <u>What is True Wealth</u>: *An anthology of essays inspired by a conversation with the Dalai Lama*).

気　気　気

From Monster To Man
by
Andrew Hazell - Aberdeen Aikido Yuishinkai - Scotland - 1st Dan

I was an angry and overactive child and started playing rugby at the age of seven, as it was a good way to vent my energy and rage. As I got older, the same rage remained and it bubbled over whenever I lost at anything. On such occasions I would become tense and pessimistic. I hated everything and the world seemed dark and grey. Looking back on it now it seems ridiculous that losing at anything could make me feel that way. On the rugby field I let it all go, vented every drop of that rage into the game, into the next tackle, into the next ruck. Off the field I focused this hyper aggression into the gym or into running. The only area where this did not work was in my aikido practice and this frustrated me.

However, even though I felt annoyed at coming off second best when practising with someone physically smaller and obviously more relaxed than me, I kept coming back. Aikido was something I couldn't beat by just using brute strength or intimidation. I didn't seem to be winning, but I was damned if I would admit defeat. Time and again though I found that anger simply did not work, and that the only person I was fighting, was myself. The thing was that I understood that this art was all about self improvement and so I knew I could not blame my difficulties on external factors. I had to look within.

A Way to Reconcile the World

Meantime, whilst struggling with aikido, rugby remained my biggest passion. It took me down a dark path that brought out in me a negative, aggressive and primal mind-set. The further I ventured down it, the worse things became. I grew more negative and broody after every defeat, on and off the field. Victories gave me little comfort, as they were never good enough or grand enough for my liking.

During the summer, when there was no rugby to be played, I tempered my body, getting ready for the following season. Focusing on my game, obsessing about how I would be the best, the toughest, and meanest. I was ready to blast the competition out of the water.

Finally I went through a season that was a complete disaster. This, of course, made me feel ever more angry and frustrated with the world and with myself. After a particular incident, it all came to a thundering halt. I found myself having to reassess my situation. It was my *sensei* who helped me through this rough time, and introduced me to *ki* breathing and *aiki* philosophy.

After this, I gave up rugby, as it now seemed trivial and unimportant and I focussed entirely on aikido, because it took me beyond winning and losing. The cloud that had been hanging over my head was suddenly lifted.

Overnight, the things that seemed so important in my childhood, now seemed silly, and were replaced with something majestic and awe-inspiring. The sky seemed bright and everything was pleasing to me. The pains I had in my shoulders and neck, due to stress slowly dissipated. Unlike at rugby training, where my shoulders hunched forwards, my head hung down and my mind was filled with aggression and anger, I found myself smiling when coming to the *dojo*, with my head held high.

Aikido totally changed the direction in which my life was heading. My friends and family noticed the difference straight away. The nice 'real' me that had been locked away by pride and ego, finally came out. I stopped causing my parents and family grief and heartache from being selfish and miserable. Instead I started to harmonise with them, and use my aikido teaching to build better relationships. I became courteous to strangers and learnt the meaning of humility. Through the discipline provided by aikido training I grew from an angry little boy into a gentle man. My reward was to meet my current girlfriend.

Aikido completely changed me and my life and has made me a much happier person as a result.

We'll Leave It at That, Shall We?
by
Simon Hirst - Jikishinkan - England - 1st Dan

Whilst venturing into the wild streets of a well-known Essex town, my friend Lee, who was an aikido student of mine, decided to park his car in one of the many relatively secure multi-storey car parks. Having found a suitable parking space he got out and locked the door behind him.

Turning around, he accidentally bumped into a man who was locking his own car. Straight away Lee apologised but the 'victim' of this 'brutal, unprovoked' attack launched a barrage of verbal abuse in response. Protesting his innocence, Lee tried to help his attacker to calm down, but without success. It became clear that the only peaceful option was to sound a retreat.

Realising his only means of escape was to move past this angry man, he attempted to do so. When Lee drew level with him though, the man grabbed his wrist and stopped him. It was one of those attacks that self-defence experts (who criticise aikido) say will 'never happen' in real life. According to Lee though, it did!

As luck would have it, only one week before, Lee and I had been practicing a basic version of *irimi nage* from *aihanmi katatedori*, where the emphasis had been on turning the hips in an attempt to blend with and neutralise just such an attack.

Well, it seems that Lee must have been paying attention, because this is pretty much what he did and the angry man slumped into a gentle, unresisting heap on the floor. Lee could have proceeded to pound his attacker into the ground, but he didn't want any trouble so as he stood over his defeated opponent, he wagged his finger and gave him some firm but fair advice. Then he turned and walked slowly away, whilst scratching his head and wondering how he'd managed to do it. The worst injury gained from the whole confrontation was a slightly dented ego.

It may be good enough to leave the story there. After all, the hero is safe, the aggressor has been vanquished and the story provides a more or less perfect illustration of aikido in action! However, barely five minutes later Lee saw the man again. He was strolling towards him up the High Street. He stopped in front of Lee and apologised. Naturally, this took Lee by surprise but he responded by saying,

"That's alright. What happened?"

He replied,

"I'd had a bad morning and you were the first person I'd met since leaving the house."

What would have happened if Lee had taken the more aggressive approach I shudder to think.

Now our *dojo*'s informal motto is Lee's parting words to his new found 'friend' and, as it happens, the last words of this story.

"We'll leave it at that shall we?"

気　気　気

Lessons from Triumph and Disaster
by
Mandakini Pokharna - Hyde Park Dojo - U.S.A. - 4th Kyu

After my sixth *kyu*, I had just learned to break fall. This ability was soon to be put to the test, as not long afterwards I went down to a lake and was walking on the rocks. I reached a point, where I could go no further and had to step back onto the grass. It was fall and pretty colored leaves were everywhere, including on the edges of the rocks and grass. What I didn't realise was that they had been blown into drifts by the wind and so when I stepped forward, what I thought was solid ground turned out to be air. Before I knew it, I was falling. Luckily, my aikido practice kicked in and I found myself doing a break fall. In so doing, I had a soft landing on the grass, rather than being dashed on the rocks. I lay all curled up, facing the sky while I regained my composure and contemplated all that had just happened. Then, smiling and enjoying the beauty of all that was around me, I got up and walked away. There was a spring in my step and gratitude for the teachings of aikido and not a hint of embarrassment!

Unfortunately, the next time something like this happened about a year later, I was not so lucky. My mind and body were not together, and so I was not present in the moment. The consequences were to provide an important lesson. Everything seemed to happen so quickly. In short, I was on my way to the bathroom and slipped. The result was a 'dislocated patella' and more than two months off work. It hurt so much that I could not move or get up on my own. I had to be helped up into a wheelchair and subsequently, even needed help to transfer myself onto the toilet seat. All very embarrassing!

One of the first things that went through my mind was, "Oh no, now I won't be able to do aikido and my exercise!" In actual fact, once I had calmed down, this turned out not to be the case, though I did have to use a wheelchair for a while. With the help of my sister, other students, and both my *sensei*, (Don Levine and Chris Galbreath), practice was adjusted in such a way that I could participate and be included!

After that initial moment, I went through the whole recovery process with a POSITIVE attitude, filled with gratitude for the chance to continue my learning, and I continued to move forward! It felt incredible to have so many people support me in this, and in fact, as a result, the accident taught me a lot. The principle lesson for me was that you have to keep going and living in the moment, no matter what blows come your way. I now count this event in my life as a blessing!

Along the way I have had many chances to practice what I have learned on the mat, off it. Aikido helps me to truly connect with others, to appreciate their point of view and to find resolutions to conflicts that have arisen. My approach to an attack is to receive it with gratitude rather than with resentment. As a result I stay relaxed and positive about my attacker and I seem to have many options. The opposite occurs when I fail.

Off the mat, I practice the religion of *Jainism*, which prescribes nonviolence, starting with conquering my own demons. I am also a Nonviolent Communication (NVC) teacher. Lessons learned on the mat are a physical embodiment of what both these other aspects of my life have to offer. I find that what I learn on the mat helps me when I am teaching NVC or helping 'young Jains,' particularly teenagers seeking to improve their relationships with their parents. They are better able to walk the line between finding themselves and benefiting from the life experience that parents bring to the table.

All in all, aikido has been life-affirming and has helped me develop into the person I am today.

How to Deal with Road Rage
by
Piers Cooke - Coldharbour Aikido Club - England - 7th Dan

About 20 years ago I was travelling to Southern France with my family, including my wife, son of six and daughter of four. At that time I was a third *dan*, aged 37, fairly fit and I guess reasonably capable.

We were joined by two other families in their respective cars and were all holidaying together. We had been driving on the auto route having crossed on the midday ferry.

We had pre-booked a number of hotel rooms just outside Lyons. This of course was in the days before satnav (GPS), so, having navigated our way down to the appropriate motorway exit, we all pulled off together as a mini convoy. It was about 7:30pm and we were all tired and hungry. We just wanted to get to the hotel, have something to eat, put the children to bed, perhaps have a quick drink and get an early night.

I was driving the second car in our little convoy, when we came to a toll. There was only one booth and exit open at this particular time and there were some seven cars in the queue. My friend Nick was two cars ahead of me and my other friend, Paul, was one car behind me. As we waited, the lights of a second toll booth switched on and it opened for business.

I pulled out, as did a French car ahead of Nick and so did the vehicle, behind me. We all lined up at the newly opened booth. The guy in front of me paid and drove off. I also paid, but because I was well ahead of my group, I pulled over to wait for the others. The vehicle that had been behind me, paid, shot out of the exit and slammed his brakes on to stop in front of me. A small Frenchman got out of the car, rushed to the left hand side of the car, where he thought the driver was, (it would have been if we were in a French car), and started yelling at us.

My wife wound down her window, and this extremely excited gentleman was shouting in French for me to get out of the car and fight. He was absolutely fuming mad. As he was shouting, flecks of spittle flew out of his mouth.

22

We all sat there absolutely amazed. Fortunately my French was good enough to understand what he wanted, which was to fight me and for me to tell him "No."

However he carried on ranting and I carried on saying "No." I even apologised for upsetting him though I had no reason to do so. In my head however, I had decided that if he touched my wife or assaulted the car that I would have to get out and for the first time in my life use what I had learnt on the mat.

I had no reason to be fearful, as firstly it was obvious that he was drunk and secondly I was substantially bigger than him, plus I felt reasonably confident in my aikido training. Anyway, it didn't come to that as he obviously realised that he had gone to the wrong car door, and shouting at my wife was getting him nowhere. Also, I think he didn't want to lose face by walking around the car and confronting me on my side. As a parting gesture, he grabbed the car door handle that he stood by, opened the door and then slammed it shut. He stormed back to his car, and sped away.

My wife and I sat there somewhat stunned by the whole escapade, still waiting for our friends to come through the other toll booth. As we sat there talking about what had just happened, a large people carrier sized police car slowly pulled up alongside us, a bit like a shark surveying its prey. The policemen looked inside the car, and I made a sign as if to say "I have no idea what that was about," and he pulled away in the direction of the mad, drunk Frenchman.

I breathed a massive sigh of relief. They had obviously been watching the whole thing. I was left with visions of what might well have happened if I had chosen to engage with this objectionable man. If a fight had ensued, he may well have been injured and then the authorities might not have been so supportive.

It was a really awful way to start a family holiday, but it could have been so much worse. Under pressure, I had stayed calm and I had done my best to calm him down by apologising for my behaviour, even though I felt I had done nothing wrong. I think he sensed my resolution and the result was that we avoided not only a fight, but potentially getting arrested.

When my friends caught up, Paul, a big guy, who had been behind us said that he had seen the whole thing and that he would have just got out and hit him.

Hooray for aikido. You can't lose a fight you don't have!

気　気　気

Unexpected Consequences
by
Hugh Purser - Cambridge Aiki Dojo - England - 1st Dan

Tokyo 1988

My teacher called me and asked for an example of how I had (successfully) applied the principles of aikido to my daily life. He was due to give a public lecture on *ki* principles and was gathering some material for his talk. So I told him of a recent exercise I had undertaken.

Remember, this is in the days long before texts, tweets and emails, but even then, there were distractions and none more so than when engaged in the main form of communication – the land line.

I had observed three things: the first was that I grabbed the phone (handset on my desk), regardless of what I was then doing, whether holding discussions with colleagues, writing research reports or checking the data monitors. Second, it took me some time, even if only a couple of seconds to focus on whomever was speaking on the other end of the line. Third, I began to notice the increased frequency with which the caller would ask, "Are you OK?" or "You sound tired". Customers and clients should feel wanted. This was clearly not helping the cause.

As a result, I experimented with an *aiki* (of sorts) technique. When the phone rang, I would let it ring a few times, and during those few seconds, I stopped whatever I was doing, focused on the phone, and most importantly focused on the person on the other end of the line, with a mindset that this was a human being I really wanted to speak to, and possibly help. This was an altogether much more positive attitude, and very quickly I noticed a change. No one asked those questions again; and customer relationships improved. My teacher liked the story so much, that a few days later, he used it in his public address.

Three months later, at another event, he was approached by a stranger, who politely introduced himself as the General Manager of the complaints department of a leading Tokyo department store.

"You don't know me" he said, "but I heard your talk three months ago; and especially the advice on how to answer a telephone. As head of the complaints department, I know when my phone rings that it will be an unhappy customer; something has gone wrong with one of the products we have sold and I have to take the blame. It was not a happy time for me, and I just was waiting for the day when I could move to another assignment, but then I tried to follow your advice. I began to welcome the ring, to imagine who might be calling, and to think that I could provide a solution. My life has changed so much for the better, and I believe the same is true for my customers too. Thank you."

気　気　気

A Spiritual Journey
by
Father Tom Plant - Cambridge Aikido - England - 1st Kyu

I started aikido in 2001, when I was at university in Scotland. Curiously, the club fell under the auspices of the Belgian Aikikai at that time.

In those days, I had no interest at all in spiritual matters; but when I left Scotland to teach English in Japan for two years, I found myself training in a *dojo* with a Buddhist monk who opened my mind to more mystical possibilities of reality than I had hitherto entertained.

This set me on a journey from atheism, through Buddhism and ultimately to Christianity, to the extent that I am now a deacon in full-time ministry in the Church of England and will next year be ordained a priest. As part of my training, I took a PhD comparing Buddhist and Christian doctrine, and have no doubt that it was the philosophy and practice of aikido that set me on this path.

The Importance of Practice
by

Jane Lott - Two Rock - U.S.A. - 3rd Dan

On December 4, 2002, my daughter Marissa and I were on the return leg of the Dipsea hike, a strenuous challenge because of extreme elevation changes over its 15-mile course. As we descended one steep ravine, Marissa said,

"Isn't it amazing how your feet know just where to go so you don't fall, the angle and speed and everything?"

"Yeah," I said. "Just like in aikido. If you stopped to think about it, it would be too late."

How many hundreds of times had I practiced getting out of the way of attackers? When you first start training in aikido, you focus on the attack.

"Oh my God," you think with an undisciplined mind, "I'm going to be hit."

Sometimes that happens, but not very hard, of course, since this is practice. But it takes many hours of such practice to learn to stop focusing on the physical attack and instead to stay relaxed enough to just get out of the way.

Then it takes hundreds more hours to learn to blend with the attack and still hundreds more learning to roll in order to protect yourself, when you are the attacker.

It's the kind of practice you do from love.

My theologist friend and I argue about this often in various forms. He says,

"God is love."

"Then God is aikido," I respond, because I love aikido passionately.

Oh, there have been many days I didn't want to practice. Days when I would come home from work and moan, "I'm too tired to go to aikido."

But my kids were wiser than I – and they loved their babysitter when they were younger; their freedom, when they were older.

"But Mom," Marissa would remind me, "just think how good you always feel when you go."

"Yeah," I would admit, and trudge off to find my gear and get to class.

That day we hiked the Dipsea was one of those bright fall days where the air was so clear we could see four or five counties from the top of Mount Tamalpais. Dried leaves crunched under our footsteps and the breeze smelled of redwoods and the hope of rain.

Lizards and skeet, which in summer rattled the underbrush, had disappeared, joining the snakes and other critters gone to earth for the winter. Deer had ventured down the mountain into landscaped back yards, searching for water and better food. The only creatures to join us on our hike that morning were an abundant variety of birds.

I remember thinking what a joy it was to share this glorious day with one of the people I love most in the world; that if I died right now, I would die happy having had this day.

I would have died that day, too, if it hadn't been for aikido.

Later that afternoon, waiting for Marissa to pick me up, I sat on the retaining wall of a sidewalk in Sausalito when, according to the police report, a Mercedes Benz driven at an excessive rate of speed ploughed into a parked pickup truck, which jumped the curb.

Hearing the sound, I turned and saw the truck barrelling at me at about 35 mph like an attacker on the mat. Instinctively, I tucked in my legs and rolled into the stairwell.

Unfortunately, the car hit the pickup at such an angle and with such momentum that it caused the truck bed to climb the stairs, bashing me on one side of the head and smashing the other side into the cement.

When I came to, I realized that had it not been for 15 years of diligent aikido practice, I would have lost my legs.

Not true, my doctor said. If it weren't for my aikido training, she said, I would have lost my life.

This is the 10-year anniversary of that crash, and my body still has not recovered. At least once a month, I endure excruciating headaches, and the bones in my neck, which took the brunt of the sheer forces, are eroding. Night terrors, which doctors say may never go away, often wake me at 4 a.m. But that's OK, aikido is a practice I can use for this, as well.

It's a metaphor for life, actually. But that's the subject for another day. In the meantime, on this Thanksgiving 10 years later, I am thankful once again to have a second chance at life. Not many people get that, and I commit once again to make good on all those promises I didn't keep the first time.

I am thankful for my children, whose love has saved my life in many ways and enriched it beyond words. And on this 10th anniversary, my life is even more blessed by the addition of a beautiful granddaughter.

I am also thankful to aikido – to O Sensei, the founder, to its teachers, practitioners and the training partners who have touched my life and brought me such strength.

I wish everyone could experience the joy at being given a second chance to live. It's especially sweet because, in a way, I earned it. Not only by putting in all those hours of hard work, but also by being willing to practice love.

Once again and with even more perception, I understand what the great statesman Benjamin Disraeli meant when he said,

"Most people go to their graves with their music still in them."

Not me. Every time I step on the mat, I'm singing.

気　気　気

A Different Response
by
A Student of Aikido of Columbus - U.S.A.

Hello, my name is John, and I've been practicing aikido for one month, and what I found out is that it's not just about self-defense: blocking, punching, throwing and rolling. It's about mind control, controlling your demeanor, which to me is really important.

One time, when I went to Wal-Mart with my wife and my grandbaby. I was coming out of the store, when I noticed from the corner of my eye this lady driving down the lane. She wasn't stopping, and I had to pull my wife back. The lady almost hit her, and as she went by, she didn't even look our way. I shouted out,

"You jerk!"

I didn't mean to say that, but I did. Her son was standing behind us, and he said,

"That's my mother you're calling a jerk, nigger."

I thought about what he said, and I thought about my *sensei* and what he had taught me. I became calm and when the lady drove back I said,

"I apologize for what I said," and we kept right on walking.

Her son looked at me kind of puzzled and so did his mom, like she wasn't expecting me to say what I said. We got in our car, went on home, no harm done. Nobody went to jail, nobody went to the hospital. My wife even gave me a high five, saying,

"I never saw you do that before, I'm very proud of you."

气　气　气

A Night on the Town
by
Nikolaos Papanikolaou - Burwell Aikido Club - England - 3rd Dan

It was a Friday night, around the beginning of October 2003. I had just finished my master's degree in physics and I was working at the University of Sussex, while training for my *shodan* grading, due in less than a month's time. As I didn't have to return to Greece for my military national service until January, I was taking the opportunity to practice hard and enjoy my few remaining months in Brighton, England. A friend and I were walking back from the *dojo* that evening and stopped at the bottom of my street to have our customary chat before we parted to our respective homes.

That night, as we were fully engaged, discussing what we had just practiced in aikido that night, a shout rang out and broke the comparative quiet. "Oi!" shouted a man from the cover of darkness. "Oi, you! I'm gonna kill you!" We both turned our heads in the direction of the voice. A man, clearly drunk, emerged from the shadows and walked in a very threatening manner towards us.

At first, we didn't realise that he was to coming for us, so we were not alarmed. However, it took only a few seconds to feel a sense of dread. Was this going to be a real fight? What should we do? Run? Fight back? As the man closed in, I realized that all of his attention and aggression was focused on my friend. I suddenly had a radical idea: I figured that as he wasn't interested in me, I had a reasonable chance of talking him out of doing something stupid. If that failed, I could always use my aikido training to immobilize him. I was scared, but I was determined.

When he was three or four paces away, I came forward and blocked the man's field of vision. "Hello!" I said with as cheerful manner as I could muster. "Can I help you?" The man stopped, but kept his attention on my friend and said,

"I am going to kill him. He attacked me!"

I asked him, "Could you please tell me what happened?"

I could feel the man's aggression diffusing a bit and thought to myself, "This is working!" The man proceeded to tell me how he had been walking to his house one night a few weeks ago, when a group of young men, roughly our age, attacked him, beat him to the ground and split his head open. He showed me his stitches. He had been roaming the streets ever since, looking for the guys that did it, as he wanted revenge. When he saw us, he thought that my friend was one of his attackers and this was his chance.

He became angry again and once more his attention was focused on my friend. My friend, apart from being third *kyu* in aikido, was also a black belt in karate, so he was also prepared for a fight, if necessary. For my part, I felt that if I could just keep talking to him in a sympathetic manner, his aggression would eventually dissipate and he would see the error of his ways.

"I am really sorry for what happened to you and you have my sympathies," I said. "I am certain that this is a total misunderstanding, because, you see, my friend only just moved into town a few days ago to start his university course. It would therefore be impossible for my friend to be your attacker because he wasn't here a few weeks ago! Could we treat this incident as a misunderstanding, go home and forget the whole thing?"

The last statement did the trick. This man seemed to sober up a bit and realized that he had made a mistake. He then turned towards my friend and apologized for his behaviour. He offered to walk us home, but as I was living with a family, I did not want to invite any sort of trouble on them, so I told him that this would not be necessary, thanked him for his kind offer and wished him a good night. He stood there for a few seconds, watching us depart the scene.

The whole experience has been burned into my psyche ever since. I was at my physical peak, and secretly, I was itching to prove that aikido technique works in sticky situations like this. However, I had chosen aikido, not just because of its self-defence potential, but because of the philosophical and moral dimensions of this particular *budo*. Didn't O Sensei himself say that aikido is the "Art of Peace?" To this day, I am still driven by the very same principles and I try to use aikido in my daily life, as for me, the real application lies outside the confines of the *dojo*.

Morihei Ueshiba used to say "*Masakatsu Agatsu Katsuhayabi*!" (True Victory is Self-Victory, may this happen at the speed of light!) He couldn't be more right!

気　気　気

An Old Head and the Young Pup
by
Kevin Jones - Shugenkai Aikido - U.S.A.

Back in the dim and distant past, when I first began practicing in the adult aikido class in my first *dojo*, there were many *yudansha* at all levels of age and ability. Since I was 16 (and not completely sane), I was quickly adopted as a "*ukemi*-puppy" by a number of them, who took great delight in bouncing me off the walls. For my part I tried to keep going until they got tired of throwing me, rather than I got tired through being thrown. In the times between *ukemi*, I'd attempt to throw my partner to the ground with as big a thud as I could arrange. All in all, just what you'd expect from a young, athletic male beginner.

There were a number of older people in the class too, but I have to admit that I tended to avoid them, because I thought that they'd be too slow and frail to be interesting. They certainly didn't seem to be bouncing off the walls!

There was one particular gentleman, Mr. Bateman, who was 86 years old at that time. He'd taken up aikido when he was about 75 and had achieved *nidan*. Although I didn't realize it at the time (what's the saying about "old heads and young shoulders not being compatible"), this person was rather special in a number of ways. He was about five feet tall, and weighed maybe 100 pounds soaking wet, but he obviously had a very strong mind. He would drive for one hour to get to class in an MGB sports car, practice for a couple of hours, go up to the bar for one drink and then drive back home again. He did this for one or two classes every week and usually practiced within a particular small group of *yudansha*. I probably assumed they were all old and slow.

One day, when I was about fifth *kyu*, I was a little slow in grabbing a partner and found myself about to practice with Mr. Bateman. I thought, "Oh well, make the best of it; take it easy on him and make sure it doesn't happen again. I'll be really careful to make sure I don't hurt him."

About 10 minutes later, I was thinking, "I wonder if I'll survive to the end of class!"

Mr. Bateman was not very physically strong but his technique was extremely powerful. I was exhausted in a matter of minutes and in a way that I never had been after an hour of full bore "blood, sweat and tears" practice with the young *yudansha*. He didn't take flying *ukemi,* but he did make dignified forward rolls and that's all anyone could make him do, no matter what their intentions were! He was efficient enough to rest in the gaps during the movements, and so was able to keep going at the same pace all night. He asked me a couple of times if I needed to rest. I think I was exhausted and in tatters long before the class ended, (but with the nicest feeling imaginable since this was clearly a gentle man in all ways). I finished the class in something of a haze.

After we finished and thanked our partners, I sat in the *dojo* for a while, thinking about what had happened, and how blind I'd previously been. I think this was probably the moment when I first realized some small glimmer of the depth in aikido. I understood that an 80 year-old really could be 'better' than a 20 year-old and that I could still be improving in my practice 70 years from that point.

It certainly helped to remove some of my arrogance and maybe helped change some of my stupidity too. I had heard people talk about *ki* before, but now I saw that it really did mean something in actual practice. I didn't know what, but it was obvious that some people had something that I didn't, and it wasn't bigger muscles.

This experience gave me a completely new approach to my practice. I still enjoyed bouncing off the walls just as much, but I began to see the differences between those who were just using force to "throw" and those who were, to whatever level, truly trying to practice aikido, with all that this entailed.

Thereafter, I went out of my way to practice with anyone, young or old, since I had discovered that there were many different approaches to practice and if I paid attention, I could benefit from any of them. I began to see the difference between just technique and aikido; I began to see the difference between a "*Do*" and self defence. I began to get a clue about why I was spending 20 plus hours each week wearing strange pyjamas and where I could go, if I continued. Oh, and I saw just how often I could insert myself into that group of 'old, slow and frail' *yudansha*.

Now maybe I would have found this out eventually anyway, but Mr. Bateman was such a graphic illustration of how wrong my thinking was, that I'm sure he saved me years at the very least. I'll always be very grateful for that, and feel blessed that there was such a person available in the *dojo* who could give this me this lesson in this way.

気 気 気

True Victory is Victory Over Oneself
by
Lila Feingold - Aikido of Santa Cruz (formerly North Bay Aikido) - U.S.A.

Running in the dark during Winter Training didn't sound so bad, since I didn't want people to see how slow I am and how long it takes me to do what everyone else seems to do effortlessly. The familiar voices in my head kept the same monotonous pace.

"Last again...just like school all over again...last one to be picked...last one to finish."

Imaginary snickers or pitying looks awaited me, I was sure, as I finally arrived back at the *dojo* defensively angry and ready to kill the first person who said anything. That person turned out to be Alan, one of the black belts, who came up to me, smiled, and he said,

"You're so brave to be doing this."

気　気　気

Aikido and Creative Expression in Music
by
Bill Levine - U.S.A.

"Morihei Sensei had a certain tension in him whenever he took up the brush, I think because he always expressed his entire being through the tip of the brush. Using the ink as a medium, he transferred his ki into the characters as he brushed them. Look at his works today and you can immediately sense the amazingly strong ki imbued in them."
Seiseki Abe Sensei, 10th Dan

Seiseiki Abe Sensei was an *uchi-deshi* for O Sensei and had the honor of teaching him calligraphy for 15 years. Apparent to Abe Sensei was how O Sensei's aikido practice had produced ways of being that guided and informed his creative expression in a powerful, aesthetic, and meaningful way.

In my experience with music as a form of creative expression, I similarly noticed aikido's extraordinarily strong influence on my creative development and expression. The embodied wisdom and awareness gained from the practice of aikido flowed naturally, almost inevitably, into my artistic process as a pianist and composer.

Between 1994-2000, I instilled the basics of aikido into my music while living in New York City, an ideal context for creative growth. Surrounded by the city's torrent of artistic passion and talent, I improvised for virtuoso modern dancers on John Cage's piano, as Merce Cunningham sat 30 feet from me. I was in the presence, as it were, of two icons of the 20th century avant-garde. I also worked at the Juilliard School with its regal and seductive Steinways, and did jazz gigs. I would like to share here some of the understanding I have gained as a musician by following the aikido path.

"Learn to understand with your body. Do not engage in a futile effort to learn a great number of techniques but rather study the techniques one by one and make each your own." - O Sensei

Budo & Piano

Traditionally, both the martial path and artistic paths incorporate a way of being that accumulates refinement by practice. In Japan, such artistic traditions as calligraphy (*shodo*), flower arrangement (*kado*), and tea ceremony (*chado*) are considered paths as worthy as any martial art path (*budo*).

Aikido can also be seen as an artistic improvisation, similar to Western fine arts, particularly "time-based arts" such as music and dance. Time-based artists are essentially processes which create phrases of energy in time and space. (*Buto* dancing or *chado* can also be seen as time-based arts, albeit at extremely slow tempos.)

It can be said that there are generally two contrasting intentions that can be expressed through the creative process: 1) the ego-oriented or secular intention, and 2) the spiritual or sacred intention. Simply put, ego-oriented art focuses mostly on the artists' personal form and style of creative expression. This type of art requires an audience for feedback, admiration, and remuneration. The artist attempts to 'do something' with an agenda to fit into cultural expectations and contexts. Although they often aim at it or inspire the transcendent, the intention is not always focused there.

Spiritual-oriented artists try to eliminate agenda and role-playing as much as possible and open to a creative experience greater than the artist. The impetus for the art arises from their unique soul, higher intelligence, and heart. The muses simply flow through them like wind and water.

Of course, a wide gray area connects the two artistic polarities. Some commercial musicians, for example, are lucky to be spiritual and have professional careers, although these days, music and art have become highly commercialized. But what I'm exploring is not what is good art or bad art. I am asking what is beneficial for the artist. What is the function of one's artistic intention?

A limitation of ego-oriented arts is that they do not intrinsically promote spiritual cultivation as part of the artist's process. In pursuing goals of competition, fame, and the attention of critics, one becomes more focused outwardly for inspiration and direction. The artistic process becomes more about honing specific skills, much like a craftsman or plumber. This is why, to get away from this orientation, in cultures as diverse as early Chinese, Indian, African and Japanese, one humbly studies with a master. The master helps the artist look for the channelled inspiration that emerges from mastering an art. For example, the early Chinese practiced a stringed instrument that was never even performed in public. It was specifically used for spiritual cultivation.

In Japan, the concept of mastery has also been well understood; there are masters ranging from paper making to sword making, and in the fine arts, masters in every area. Stemming from this tradition, masters such as O Sensei and Abe Sensei found a confluence between fine arts and martial arts. Since I had learned aikido in a traditional Japanese way from Matsuoka Sensei and Abe Sensei, I eventually began to see the study of piano improvisation as a path.

Aiki & Harmony

Aikido enables the body to viscerally appreciate the nature of conflict and harmony, a polar tension important in every art. As I applied my aikido training to music, I was better able to physically feel the varying degrees of harmonic tension, resonating within my torso, skull, and bones, as resonant frequencies moved around and away from a tonal center. (When singing in the shower, the "boom" spot is a resonant frequency.) Tonal center, like *hara*, is a place from which music springs, journeys, and to which it eventually returns. Through aikido I learned that the core of musical harmony and melody resides within the resonant frequency tensions in the body, *ki* field and emotions as music moves towards or away from center. I concluded that harmonic experience embodies a continuous gesture rooted in the expansion and contraction of energy, corresponding to a present awareness of tone.

Aikido practice heightened this musical understanding. After a few years of diligent concentration on music, I could finally truly experience harmony. When I listened to familiar music I was able to now feel the harmonic gestures and understand them as if for the "first time." When I read new pieces, I deeply absorbed them on a harmonic level, and my musical ear rapidly improved.

Bowing & Posture

Here I'm not talking about the wooden bow a fiddler uses on his instrument! Rather, the aikido-derived concept of respect and reverence for being able to practice your art, and being happy that human beings can express themselves. I created a ritual of preparing myself. I showed up early for gigs and stretched. I cleared my mind as much as possible. I assumed good posture on the bench. I made sure that I was at the most ergonomic height for my forearms and that I was at the correct distance (*ma'ai*) from the piano, as if it were my training partner.

Before and during playing, aikido body and wrist stretches are very effective for piano playing. Also, balancing and calming my energy field back/front, up/down, and left/right in the style of Wendy Palmer's embodied awareness. All this changed my relationship with the piano, drawing it closer to me and into a new feeling of intimacy with music.

"Ueshiba Sensei's spirit resides in his calligraphy not in the forms or shapes of the characters, but in their resonance and light. Similarly, that spirit resides in aikido not in the techniques you can see with your eyes, but in those you cannot." - Abe Seiseki Sensei

Center

The effect of starting with a focus on bowing and posture is emotional balance and equanimity. The heart is more open and compassionate; there is less anger and adrenaline; the energy is feeding back into the heart. This is a calm, stable place to begin creative expression. The heart is 'centered.'

At the same time, I utilized the physical center found in *hara*. This comes from years of aikido practice focusing on center. So when I use the word "center," I mean from the heart (love), the belly (power), and the earth (ground).

I now realize that during the act of creative expression, being centered is a *choice* if one is mindful. Sustaining the choice requires vigilance and focused awareness, especially with master dance teachers who have a better sense of time than most musicians. Dancers taking a class can transfer to musicians a physical and energetic nervousness and excitement, and I often found myself losing center. I would realize I was off when I forced ideas, expressing overly emotional and inappropriately loud music. Adrenaline kicks in and the tempo naturally speeds up further and further. Non-centered artistic expression becomes stressful and I play wrong notes. The antidote to losing my mindfulness and awareness is to re-center myself by aligning my posture, breathing, focusing on my *hara*, and opening the heart. Once centered, I can be more sensitive and open to musical potential.

In one class the dancers were all excited that Mikhail Baryshnikov would take Merce Cunningham's company class. Their nervousness and excitement was contagious, and I became stampeded with emotions and the tempo increased. The master Baryshnikov walked over to the piano, as strong and grounded as a lion, and simply draped his arm on the piano. I got the message, and quickly re-centered and contained the tempo.

In aikido, non-centered anxiety produces techniques that at best don't work, and at worst, injure others. Being centered requires practice within one's technical ability level. Once I'm not overly self-involved, I can then extend my attention to the creative context while playing: to musicians, dancers, the audience, and the room itself. Just as one does not want to "fight the flowers" in *ikebana*, one wants to blend with his or her own instrument and with other musicians and dancers.

While one is centered, creativity stems from a balanced source, good for playing consciously without too much passion, thus avoiding such pitfalls as sappy, angry or otherwise contrived music. I feel safe to explore a range of non-tonal music or very emotionally expressive music, knowing how it will manipulate the body's emotions and *ki*. As a film composer, I am also more keenly aware of how music will affect others emotions and the activity on the screen.

"Dance is an art in space and time. The object of the dancer is to obliterate that." - Merce Cunningham

Breath Power

Watching Abe Sensei do calligraphy I was struck by the variety of styles in his brushwork. He demonstrated that he could put the same type of breath power, or *ki*, into his brush as he did during aikido techniques. He could draw in the style of *irimi*, with bold lines, or he could create soft strokes on the paper, spiralling like *tenkan*. He could be specific or abstract with his breath and intention. I also noticed that he started each piece with the utmost concentration, and continued his focus until he lifted the brush off the paper with his breath and heart.

So it naturally occurred to me to practice breathing *ki* into melodies and harmony. This is when I began a period of beautiful folk piano music. I explored gentler harmonies and slower tempos. It was as though joyful music was channelling through me. To paraphrase a metaphor about ego used by Zen Master Suzuki Roshi, I was simply a screen door that would open and shut to let music through. My music was less dark, frustrated, and complex. The inspiration seemed to spring forth endlessly.

Also, at the Cunningham studio, doing soft or silent *ki-ais* to build power was extraordinarily helpful when I had 30 tired dancers at the end of class and I too was tired. Arousing *ki* helped to create strong, earthy, bass-heavy musical energy that buoyed the dancers.

The dancers, who are often absorbed in themselves and their class, for the first time began to give me compliments. One dancer showed me how helpful my music was by placing her hand supportively on my lower back. "This is how your music feels," she said. The harmonies were less ambiguous and more accessible to the dancers. Another dancer remarked how beautiful my music was sounding.

Technique

I was able to focus on piano technique from the same sincere approach used to improve my aikido technique. I discovered through aikido, and with the help of a Juilliard pianist, a central secret to piano technique: relax. As soon as my wrists tense, phrases sound clunky. When my body tenses and the breathing halts, musical creativity stops. The trick is to blend with the piano, as in aikido we blend with training partners.

In aikido (and dance), I have heard that to maintain balance one can continually expand the body in all directions. Likewise, in music it's important to expand *ki* into the instrument so as not to become technically rigid. Through relaxation and expansion, based on aikido principles, I began to create music that flowed like a river; phrases connected, and I played longer without fatigue. Since I was playing a total of 15-20 hours a week, these techniques became embedded.

"To compensate for their difficulties they do what almost everybody does in this art: They force when they should flow, hurry when they should wait, and tighten instead of relaxing. To their bewilderment, they are finding that aikido is not something one succeeds in by being stronger; and it's not just one more sport you can simply figure out and do. It's a complete re-programming in mind, body, and spirit." - Richard Strozzi-Heckler

Flexibility

While practicing in New York, I realized that there are many adventures in music if one utilizes the flexibility learned from aikido. As I mentioned before, harmonies are a journey from home, the tonal center, to a chord that is away from center, and then, perhaps back. The harmonic variations depend on whether the harmony wants to wander off constantly (chromatics), go far away (modulation), or stay close to home (drone tonality). Too much modulation disorients the listener. This is interesting for listening and playing, but for dancing, people like to stay around a tonal center. This is why most popular dance music has few chords (such as merengue, or rap, electronica, and folk music).

Only when I consistently practiced over years did I approach mastering flexibility and was willing to take side routes and detours on my harmonic journeys. I can now quickly maneuver through polarities: yin/yang, tension/relaxation, suspension or ambiguous harmony/resolution, fast/slow rhythms within tempos, complexity/simplicity, high harmonic colors/low colors, and soft/loud dynamics. And I don't worry where the voyage is going, I'll get there when I get there, playing in control but loose, less afraid and less attached to results.

"The only way to do it is to do it." - Merce Cunningham

Authenticity & Honesty

One of the goals of making art a path seems to be authentic creative expression. I learned that when you sit down to create, be sure you "don't know" what you are going to do. There was more of a sense of relaxation to my music (supported by my more relaxed technique) and I was less driven. The music had its own innate vitality without me having to coerce, force, or coddle it. The Zen "Don't know mind" is crucial for musical honesty and authenticity. When I asked Abe Sensei "what was O Sensei like as a student?" when he instructed him in *shodo,* Abe Sensei told me: "Like a blank page." Music can have honesty if you don't over use what you know, getting out of the way, so that new music can bubble up. If you create a piece and overwork it, then it will lose honesty. It becomes contrived and loses freshness.

After a while, my left hand surprisingly was playing all kinds of new techniques because I was practicing so much and absorbing the NYC creative inspiration. For a period almost all that I played was authentic. But then that stopped and I was back to only about 80% authentic. I think a direct path to my authenticity happens when I explore the essentials of music. What is essential harmony and rhythm? What is folk music and minimalist music? What are the impacts of bass lines when you begin with them?

Cunningham demonstrated that one cannot be too simple. I would sometimes start with one note and go from there. I'd wait to see what would arise. The trick was not to copy someone else's style or a cultural norm. Copying creates dishonest, contrived creativity. So I borrowed Cunningham's practice discipline of each day going over what you know, and then adding on to it something fresh. This is how one can develop new ideas and a wider vocabulary in an authentic, centered way.

Artistic Completeness

Combining aikido in musical practice, finding your true voice, can lead to finding your unique expression, your own artistic completeness.

Looking back at this period of my life I can now see the overall function was to develop my authentic voice and artistic completeness. It will still take me years but that's because I love complexity. For another artist it may be one single unique form of expression. No one plays music your way so there is no need to compare and to compete.

気 気 気

Stair Surfing and Billiard Brilliance
by
Tom Simpson - Aikido of Floyd - U.S.A. - 2nd Dan

Here is an unbelievable *aiki* moment that happened one morning at home.

I was barefooted, carrying a heavy piece of luggage down the stairs. With luggage in one hand, and a few bits and pieces in the other, I went down three steps. Then I stopped, so I could lean back and pick up another object from the top step that I wanted to take with me. It was just a little too far, because the wheels on the luggage caught the step and the case took off down the stairs. My feet slipped out from under me. Amazingly, I remained calm and centered. Time slowed way down. Without letting go of the luggage or the other stuff and using a combination of my elbow resting on the banister and working with the sliding case, I successfully surfed the stairs, all the way to the bottom!

The cool thing was that I was aware of how I lowered my center and shifted it forward, so that I gained a semblance of control, maneuvering my feet so they struck every one of the nine foot strikes on the way down, which helped slow me down. At the bottom, I came to a stop in full control of my balance, still holding everything. My first thought, standing there astonished and pleased, was "Thank you, aikido."

My other life is teaching billiards. Once I was in Virginia Beach with Tommy Jones, my assisting billiard instructor, who is a long-time karate teacher.

We were walking around with his wife in the area of the resort town most frequented by tourists. It was Friday night, and very crowded. Suddenly, he noticed a lot of people gathering. He realized a fight was about to break out. Tommy quickly wiggled his way to the front of the crowd, where he could see that the fight was seconds from beginning.

Sure, he could have jumped in and used his karate skills to break it up, but that likely would have ended with people hurt, possibly a bigger brawl, and maybe a police incident. Instead, he did an amazing, *aiki* thing. He jumped into the conflict circle and began break dancing on the ground next to the action! The crowd loved it, and the fight immediately dissolved. Another wonderful *aiki* moment!

I earned my *nidan* at Aikido of Columbus under Paul Linden Sensei, (a wonderful, life-changing experience). For the last seven years, I've been teaching at my own *dojo* in Virginia, Aikido of Floyd. I have to credit Paul and aikido training for helping me gain the awareness, balance, and presence that saved my rear that day on the stairs. As I like to tell my students, we're not training for the day when a roving band of ninjas attacks us in a back alley of our town. Among many things, we're improving our ability to survive the kinds of things that happen in daily life, like falling on stairs.

気 気 気

An Aiki Soldier

by

Richard Strozzi-Heckler - Two Rock - U.S.A. - 6th Dan

I first met Birks when he was recently promoted to First Lieutenant, just a year out of The Basic School. He was the officer who supported our efforts running the Marine Warrior Project, the precursor to the Marine Corps Martial Art Program (MCMAP) at Camp Pendleton in 2000. In his support position he was close to the project, but wasn't a direct participant, yet he was intensely interested and hounded me daily about what we were doing.

He was a Division 1 collegiate wrestler in college and had tried a number of martial arts. He was tough, disciplined, and carried a big heart in his barrel chest. I would show him what we were doing and he would hang around as much as his time allowed. He was a solid Marine and cared about his men, and thought what we were doing would help his Marines. At some point I gave him the names of some aikido *dojos* in the area and he began training.

Over the years, I would get emails from Lt. Birks from around the world, and he said he was continuing his aikido training wherever he went.

Then I heard a story about a Marine officer near Falluja, Iraq, who had his patrol drop to one knee, take their helmets off, and bow their heads as an Iraqi funeral procession passed by. This diffused a potentially dangerous moment as the funeral crowd was outraged seeing an American unit patrolling nearby and they made threatening gestures.

Later the Iraqis spoke of the officer's virtues in how he respected their culture. Coincidence or not, Captain Birks' unit suffered minimal casualties in their deployment in this area. Later when I asked Birks about this he simply said,

"It seemed like the *aiki* thing to do."

気　気　気

One Dance

by

Mary McLean - Centerfield Aikido - U.S.A.

One day when I was in third grade, I came back from recess early, by myself. When I walked into the empty classroom, there was Sandy Epstein, the biggest kid in the class, standing alone on the far side of the room with a dark look on her face. She looked up and saw me instantly. There was no escape. Sandy had been systematically beating up on all the kids in the class, just because.

I was one of the few she hadn't yet encountered. She was twice my size, or so it seemed. Because of her unreasoned intent to 'get' people, the second we glanced at each other I knew it was all over, in terms of my being able to evade her. I was an only child, with no idea of how to fight with siblings. No one was around. I knew that if I ran, she and others would hunt me down on the playground as an easy mark. Leaving was not an option.

I suddenly felt light and giddy. An unforeseen wave of this lightness carried me into the room and made me act in a strangely positive way. I realized that I had to turn the tide and be the one in charge. She started for me from the corner of the room, with her arms outstretched. I thought she looked like Frankenstein lurching toward me with an almost trancelike motion. For a moment I didn't know what to do. Then I saw her arms and they reminded me of grown-ups when they are dancing. So, just as she got to me, I raised both my arms, rested my hands gently on her upper arms, and said,

"Let's dance!"

Our faces were about two feet apart. Hers took on this gradually dawning look of astonishment. I led her around the room as if we were ballroom dancing in a great spirit of joviality. Love welled up inside me, at first as an act to convince her to change her mind, but then as a true feeling of gentle protection toward this other girl. Sandy smiled, and we danced all over the room.

She never bothered me again. We always smiled and waved "Hi!" to each other on the way to school. One dance had been enough.

気　気　気

Aikido as a Medicine

by

Reesa Abrams - Aikido of Santa Cruz - U.S.A. - 5th Kyu

In May, 1995 I woke up from a 13-day coma. I was told that the doctors did not know exactly what was wrong with me. It seemed that as I was getting older, I was getting progressively more ill. I could never hold onto physical fitness. Now I was an asthmatic. They thought I might have multiple sclerosis and I faced the prospect of never working again and indeed, never walking again.

In the first weeks after the coma, I hallucinated a lot because of the drugs I was on. In one these episodes I recall a vision in which one of the medical doctors who looked after me was telling me, that I would be okay because I could take aikido and it would make me better. This seemed strange because I did not know what aikido was. Later on, when I found out it was related to the martial arts, I laughed. I could not do that!

In November, 1995 I was diagnosed with extreme mercury toxicity. The prognosis was not good. I looked for information on the internet and what I discovered made me sob. I had 12 silver amalgam fillings in my mouth that were leaching mercury into my blood. Not only did I have it, but I had passed it to my daughter through the placenta.

In May, 1996, despite another shorter coma of only 24 hours, which meant that I had to move from living in the country in La Honda to the town of Santa Cruz, so that I could be closer to the doctors who were treating me, I was on the road to recovery. My condition was still pretty serious. I was taking a lot of pharmaceuticals, which had their own special set of side effects. I could now walk again, but physical strength was not present. It had a profound effect on me both spiritually and emotionally.

A Way to Reconcile the World

One day in September, I was looking at the local tv channel for Santa Cruz and there was a short film about aikido, featuring Linda Holiday Sensei. It provided a number to call. I picked up the phone and dialled. The phone was answered by Sensei herself. I told her of my condition and of my hallucination. She told me to come down and visit and that the next beginner's class would begin in a few weeks time. This was how I came to join what was then called North Bay Aikido, (now Aikido of Santa Cruz).

Between 1996 and 2006 I took the eight-week beginner class over and over again. It took me six months to learn how to do a backward roll from standing and two years to do a front roll from standing, despite receiving the best mentoring from many of the *sensei*.

Mercury toxicity is characterized by a lot of fear and emotional dysfunction. Some days I could only do warm-ups because I could not allow another person's energy to blend with mine, even receiving a simple grab was too much. I learned how to cope by continuing to come to the *dojo*. Some days I slept or was ill for as much as 20 hours at a time, but I kept on turning up, even if I only sat on the side and watched. Whatever I brought in the door was accepted. The *dojo* was, and still is, a safe haven.

So, how am I different? A coma is a life altering experience. Having your entire body cleansed of a systematic toxin that has been there for 40 + years is also. I was having identity crises daily between 1997 and 2006, but aikido gave me the tools to recover and to grow. I learned to: center, breath properly, blend, be decisive, act, forgive myself, and to move on. These skills have helped me deal more effectively with what life throws at me and I am a better person as a result.

For example, recently at work I had two powerful managers telling me what to do at the same time. Unfortunately, the instructions they each gave were completely at odds with each other. I was literally and metaphorically stuck in the middle of them and it was all becoming very uncomfortable. I found myself centering and I turning slightly to get off the line between them. The dynamic immediately changed and they ended up taking care of me and resolving their issues. I feel that the outcome would not have been so positive without my aikido training.

People tell me that surviving what happened to me was a miracle. I tell them that I had a lot of help. The biggest help of all was the support and compassion offered at North Bay Aikido.

One thing is for sure, when you come so close to losing it all, everyday is precious!

Sometimes It's Not Pretty

by

Tim Bamford - Test Valley Dojo - England - 1st Dan

Being a doorman can be precarious at times and you always have to be alert. Sometimes you can be threatened when your shift has ended, walking to the car or your friends or even to a different venue. The uniform sticks out in a sea of Burberry. In these instances it may become necessary to defend yourself and the results can be ugly. I recently had to use aikido in its raw form to save my life.

Walking back to my car after a fairly quiet shift I heard rapid footsteps behind me and an aggressive "Oi" (the perfect example of British etiquette). So I turned around and found myself facing three men. It was fairly obvious that they didn't want directions or a taxi number, partly because the man in front ran forwards and swung a crowbar at my head. In these moments you don't think, you act. I wouldn't be writing this now if I had thought for even a micro-second.

Unbendable arm and *ikkyo* principle, blocking the swinging arm and striking his collar bone, while directing him towards the tarmac. The second man, close behind, ended up with another extended arm across his face, spinning him and allowing me to kick his ankle as I stepped forward to meet the third attacker. I blocked and swept a punch aside, before striking him with the blade of my hand and arm, from face to shoulder. With the latter two men out of action, the first man, whilst still on the ground swung at me with the crowbar. Whilst blocking this and disarming him, I did end up breaking his arm. It was enough and I was able to go back to my car, while they limped hurriedly away. Now this lasted a maximum of 10 seconds. Everything came from natural reaction and muscle memory. Aikido's principles were extremely evident throughout this.

Maybe these guys had a problem with doormen, perhaps they mistook me for someone else or maybe they simply intended to mug me. Whatever it was, they intended me serious harm. Although the results were not pretty, I think that without my training, the situation could have been a lot worse, for me and for them. Reasonable force is a term that comes up a lot in my job. It is in fact part of the law. In my opinion, not only was this reasonable, but it was necessary.

I am certain that aikido saved my life and this incident has driven me to increase my training. I want to help others to both avoid and be prepared for similar situations.

気　気　気

Randori in Graduate School
by
Paul Linden - Aikido of Columbus - U.S.A. - 6th Dan

All the way through high school and college, I maintained a steady 2.0 average. Looking back on it, I really didn't know how to study effectively. However, that changed drastically in graduate school.

To begin with, I resolved that I would do the homework the day it was assigned. After years of putting off homework until the last minute, I finally realized that such an approach may not have been the best way to absorb the material I was studying.

I remember sitting in class the first day of my graduate program, hearing the first homework assignment, and going right off to the library to do it. It was 30 years ago, but I still remember the jolt of panic I felt as I ploughed into the first reading assignment.

I started reading, and two minutes into the reading I was dismayed to find that I had totally forgotten what I'd read on the first page. My first thought was that in the eight years I had been out of school, my brain had turned to mush. But some voice from within spoke up and said, "Don't sweat it! Just keep on reading." I kept on reading, and I kept on not remembering, and I kept on feeling that it would all work out somehow.

A couple of weeks later, I walked into one of my classes only to find that a major test had been scheduled while I was out with the flu the week before. I figured I'd flunk the test since I had not studied for it, and with that on my mind, I began. However, I was surprised to find that when I read the first question, all the relevant material from the readings popped back into my mind with a clarity and precision I had never experienced before. And it was the same way for all of the questions. Later on, I found that I had achieved a nearly perfect score on the test.

At first it seemed puzzling to me, but on reflection I began to understand what had happened. I realized that I had been studying with the same mental focus with which I practiced aikido *randori*. *Randori* is the practice of defending against a group attack. There are two important points in successful *randori*. The first is that you are not a victim. You are actually in charge of what happens. I express this to my aikido students by saying that the defender is bait. The attackers will rush to follow you wherever you go, and so thinking of yourself as bait, you can lead a group of attackers where you want them to go.

The second point is that you have to pay attention in a very special way. I express this to my students by saying that you have to put the first 100% of your attention on the attacker who is currently closest to you, and you put the second 100% on all the other attackers. The mathematics may be questionable, but that's really what it's like. It's not a balance of narrow-beam attention versus broad-field attention. It's doing both simultaneously. And to do this, you have to be placid and clear, with your attention anchored inside you and focused outside you. It's like being a still pond reflecting the sky, but far more active than that. Because of this special state of mind, you are able to take in all the details of the fast-paced and sometimes chaotic situation and make effective decisions about what to do. You throw one attacker to the ground and move on to the next. Your total attention switches from the first attacker to the second, but a part of your attention stays on the first attacker to make sure he isn't

51

getting up again, and another part of your attention is devoted to the group as a whole.

That was the state of mind in which I was studying. It allowed me to input the material much more efficiently. And the sense I had of forgetting what I just read, that was my attention leaving what I had just read and moving on to what I was reading next. At the end of my M.A. and Ph.D. programs, I had about a 3.98 average.

I began my graduate program with one *randori*, and I ended it with another. My dissertation defense was indeed a group attack. Now you have to realize that though I was receiving a degree in Physical Education, my actual area of interest and study was somatic education. In other words, I knew very little about sports and a lot about body awareness.

I arrived 45 minutes early at the room where the examination was to be held. I rearranged the tables and chairs so that there was a clear focal point to their arrangement – and I sat in that focal point. When the first member of my committee arrived, I welcomed him to my dissertation defense and invited him to take a seat. I did the same for each member of the committee as she or he arrived. In other words, I was assuming command of the social situation.

When it turned nine o'clock, I suggested that we start the proceedings. I turned to the head of my committee and invited him to ask the first question. I gave him a partial and somewhat odd answer, and of course he asked me to please amplify and explain what I just said. I did, but I also left another area of incompleteness in the answer, and so another member of the committee asked for more information in that area. In other words, I was using myself as bait to control the direction of the attackers' movements. The bottom line was that my dissertation committee could have asked me any questions about any area of Physical Education, but I kept them following me around in the subject areas in which I was most knowledgeable.

Of course, it was all friendly and respectful. The professors were on my committee precisely because they were interested in the topic of body awareness education. Nonetheless, my dissertation defense flowed smoothly in part because I took charge of the situation and kept it flowing smoothly, which was a process that I learned in aikido *randori*.

气　气　气

Skiing the Aiki Way
by
Dave Belfield - West Buckland Dojo - England - 5th Kyu

In March 2012, my son, Andrew Belfield was an eight-year old with an orange stripe belt when he went on his second family skiing holiday to Les Arcs 2000, in France. He had a little experience on skis, but was really looking forward to making good progress this time and being able to ski with his family.

When my family arrived at the resort, we were incredibly lucky to have fresh snow and excellent conditions. Andrew was very keen to get going and joined a small group of similar ability English children with an English-speaking French Ecole du Ski Francais ski instructor. The first day was uneventful, with Andrew perfecting his snowplough and moving off the nursery slopes, much to his delight.

Day two was unfortunately a different story. He was following the instructor down a narrow and quite steep incline coming back into the village, when his ski tips crossed and he lost control. For a moment he managed to uncross his skis, but this only made matters worse as he picked up a dramatic amount of speed very quickly.

The ski instructor was unable to catch Andy as he hurtled past and could only look on, in horror, as he plummeted towards the bottom of the slope. In desperation Andy threw himself into an aikido roll, tucking in tight, as he hurtled past startled skiers, crashed through not just one, but two crash fences and ended up on the road, luckily without any traffic coming.

Within seconds, childcare staff reached him, closely followed by a very worried ski instructor. Everyone was amazed when he sat up, dusted himself off and said, "I'm OK." The only injuries were a couple of bruises on his legs where his skis had come off in the fall. The instructor had never seen anyone with so few injuries from what she described as a "very serious fall." He was back skiing the next day, and got his wish to ski down the mountain by the end of the week with his family.

We all swear that if he had not known how to roll properly through his love of aikido, things would have turned out very differently. Andrew is now an orange belt with West Buckland Aikido Club, and owes a lot to his fantastic sensei Vince Lawrence.

Thanks Vince!!

気　気　気

Late One Night
by
David Gross - 2nd Dan - U.S.A.

It was late one night and I was walking home down a wide, well lit, deserted sidewalk. It ran past a Chevy dealership. Walking in my direction were two fellows and though they were a ways off, they gave the impression being inebriated from the sway of their shoulders and elbows as they walked. They looked as if they wanted trouble by the way they were punching and kicking the cars and trucks as they went past.

They were on the right side of the sidewalk as they approached me. I moved to my left, hoping the gap of nine or so feet would be protection for me. As they drew close, one of the fellows approached me. He raised his hand to strike me. My aikido training stayed with me. Up to that point, even with all the tension in the air, I hadn't cringed and I hadn't become aggressive.

His hand descended toward my head and I reached and took it and shook his hand. He sort of jumped.

"Um, how's it going?" he blurted out.

We exchanged pleasantries and continued on our respective ways.

That was my aikido at its best. I didn't over-react. I didn't anticipate or try to force the situation. The violence was safely diffused. It happened without thought or planning. My heart was in my throat and its pounding was loud in my ears all the way home.

気　気　気

Falling Down and Getting Up
by
Cath Riddoch - Kannon Aikido Club - Scotland

Only during the last few years have I realised that the best lesson I learned from aikido is at least partially a manifestation of an old Zen saying "nana korobi ya oki," meaning 'get knocked down seven times, get up eight times.' It is essentially about not giving up, but more than that, for me, it was about learning to stay engaged with the process that was knocking me down. I learned not to turn away and to stay connected, feeling for the opening or opportunity to regain my balance.

It happened when I was training at a seminar with a visiting *sensei*, who is now a *shihan*. I was a 5th *kyu* at the time and we were doing *ikkyo*. As *uke*, as soon as my balance was compromised I fell to the floor. *Sensei* told me, "*Uke* never dies." He showed me and let me feel the difference between *uke* falling to the floor and *uke* staying alive. People talk about such moments as being like a light turning on, and for me, it really was just like that. Suddenly I understood. The class was called to line up and to my disbelief, rather than asking for one of his usual *ukes*, *Sensei* asked for me. I was terrified! Before this moment, I had never been used as *uke* by any *sensei* ever. Now here I was standing in front of a whole seminar, about to be *uke* for this really important *sensei*. He demonstrated *ikkyo* and as he applied the technique, I felt utterly connected, as if we were tied together. He demonstrated the connection by moving up and down several times before releasing me back to the line up and calling for his usual *uke*.

From that point on, as *uke*, I never just 'die.' I stay with the technique and to try to feel for an opportunity to get up. At the time, I knew I had learned something important and was also really amazed that it was me who had been used as *uke* in front of everyone. However, it was not until much later that I fully understood the significance of what I had learned.

About a year after the lesson in 'not dying,' I had my first major episode of what turned out to be multiple sclerosis (MS). Since that time, I go through periods of relapse and remission. When I am ill, I lose control of half my muscles, experience all manner of unimaginable horrors and eventually emerge exhausted with only a fraction of my body working.

It is at this point after every relapse, the low point, where once again I feel like I have lost everything. It is then, metaphorically when my bum is on the ground, that I remember the lesson learned.

I know that 'not getting up' is simply not an option. I start to feel for the opportunity to get up. If that is only moving a finger, then I move it, and remain searching for the next opportunity. After five major relapses I know the pattern well. I can let myself crash to the floor of relapse now with some degree of grace, if not a little anguish. I follow my *tori* faithfully, knowing that I will get up from it. That is what I trained to do, to fall gracefully, I then get up. No thought, no choice, no turning away from the pain.

After 10 years at the same *kyu* grade I decided it was time to change clubs. I went through a difficult time of re-learning and discarding much of what I previously believed to be true. It was only when I came to discard the belief that *uke* should always be trying to get up that I appreciated the depth of emotion associated with it for me. It was then that I saw how much of an impact that one lesson, thirteen or fourteen years previously, had had on me and the way I deal with MS.

To be accepted in the new club, it seemed I had to discard even my most treasured belief, as their method of learning involves training with pauses. Getting up mid-technique is considered bad form since it would exploit the teaching methodology, which is not present in the final flowing technique. Nevertheless, the attitude of 'get up, get up, get up, no matter what,' had been so ingrained in me over the years and was now so much a part of my core being that even when I fall to the mat with no attempt to get up, now my mind and spirit remain connected. I no longer turn away in fear, because I know, deeply and confidently, it is possible to face even the fiercest attack. What I have learned physically on the mat has made its way deep into my being.

Each relapse leaves me with more lasting damage to my nervous system and as a result more disabled. In the recovery from one relapse, it was looking as if I might become a permanent wheelchair user. I had forced things too soon and damaged my knee from walking on it when I had insufficient strength or muscle control. It was a very dark time for me. I reached a new level of dysfunction wherein it seemed logical, even to the medics, to give up and stop trying to do the impossible. I distinctly remember thinking to myself that I had been a bad *uke*, I had fought the recovery, resisted what the MS was doing to me. When I became aware of this, I regained my patience and did only what I was able to do, whilst all the time looking for that opportunity to get up. Eventually the opportunity came and gradually, with fewer and fewer braces, supports and sticks, I could walk further and further.

Don't worry, I'm not delusional. I know that no matter how much aikido and *zazen* I do, there is no state of mind that can 'win' or prevent this terrible condition from eventually taking my body piece by piece, even if it is still a game of tug-of-war at the moment. The beauty is in knowing I can deal with it, however cruelly it attacks me. This capacity to deal with the rapid deterioration and the grief of loss for things I used to do, comes from aikido.

When I stop for a moment and think about my situation it really scares me, but I'm not running from the truth! I am able to face it, to be present and to feel it fully. The thousands of times I've been thrown to the mat and got back up again have ingrained something deep inside me. It is a reflex now. One day, maybe after my next relapse, I will be unable to practice on the mat ever again, but the will and spirit polished over years of training will stay with me and I will search for opportunities to get up in whatever way I can.

This has been aikido's gift to me.

気　気　気

Along the Aiki Road
by
Jamie Leno Zimron - U.S.A. - 5th Dan-

Stanford, Winter Break, 1975 - Coming from the Midwest, I hadn't even heard of martial arts or eastern culture when my girlfriend first told me about aikido. She was already a blue belt and talked about this flowing practice of harmonious power, where the teacher spoke in metaphors about nature and moved like a ballet dancer. Then she described an almost idyllic atmosphere of cooperation instead of competition in class.

It all sounded way too good to be true. So when Winter Quarter started and I could get a college Physical Education credit for aikido, I went with some cynicism to check it out. But I discovered that it was even better than she had said. Soon we were both at Stanford noon class with Frank Doran *Sensei* five days a week, plus Woodside High (the seed of Aikido West) or the Turk Street *dojo* in San Francisco, later in the day.

I remember Joan Baez singing at *Sensei's* wedding, and heading up "Blue Belts Forever"; an overflowing mat and George Leonard taking his *shodan* exam at Saotome *Sensei's* first seminar at Stanford. And thinking that Doran *Sensei's* magnificent movement and teaching were truly "Beethoven aikido."

Berkeley 1978 - Mutual friends introduced me to a wonderful group of tradeswomen because they were martial artists. They had started going out to a rustic camp in the Sierras, to train and learn about the way-cool stuff everyone was doing. It was just awesome to discover kung fu and t'ai chi from China, shotokan karate and judo from Japan, and taekwondo and kuk sul won from Korea. These tradeswomen were tough and thought aikido was lovely with nice ideas, but didn't really believe that it was very effective for self-defense.

One evening, we were all sitting around when the barrage of 'what if' questions started: What if you get punched, or kicked, or choked, or attacked like this or like that ... ??? I was a baby brown belt, and a black belt karateka suddenly got up and started coming at me. There was no chance to prepare or even think. Thankfully, my body had enough training in it to do things like move off the line, enter, swirl around, extend my hand into her face or solar plexus. Much to all our amazement, she kept falling down, and I never got hit or hurt. We realized then that aikido was more than pretty. *It really works!*

Russia 1987 - Koichi Barrish *Sensei* led a group of 35 *aikidoka* on the first foray into the Soviet Union, where martial arts had been banned under communism as too empowering to 'the people.' This was still the early days of Gorbachev, glasnost ('opening-up') and perestroika ('re-structuring'). That first trip felt like going into the gulag. Airport personnel were all uniformed soldiers. We were required to stay in state-run hotels, keep our receipts from state-run banks, and often had our cameras confiscated. Most *keiko* sessions were conducted in clandestine meeting places.

We did get to work with a sanctioned Olympic judo club that the state wanted to show off. Then, near the end of our trip, somehow the doors of Moscow University were opened to us after literally being shut in our faces earlier. Both sides, American and Russian, were equally nervous and excited to meet. The Russians fell in love with aikido (who wouldn't?!), which allowed us to fall in love with one another, and soon, so many stereotypes fell away and rapprochement began.

O Sensei's vision of aikido as a "great way to reconcile the world and make all human beings one family" was taking form as a wonderful tool in the burgeoning Citizen's Diplomacy movement, creating new friendships and social change through direct people-to-people contact.

West Bank 1994 - After the Oslo peace accords were signed in 1993, up until Israeli Prime Minister Yitzhak Rabin was assassinated in late 1995, there seemed to be some real hope for resolution of the Mideast conflict. I was living in Jerusalem and had my first opportunity to go to the West Bank and Gaza, through the Compassionate Listening Project led by Leah Green. We met with a wide spectrum of Israelis and Palestinians, religious and secular. Hearing their stories. Listening in Palestinian villages and Jewish settlements. Talking with ordinary people and political leaders. Witnessing the Occupation and seeing what we could do to help build bridges and end the violence.

Leah appreciated aikido, so at times included *aiki* 'peace somatics' in our meetings. Everyone loved how aikido provided physical as well as verbal ways to interact compassionately. Working in structured *aiki*-pairs and practices helped combatants bypass separation and connect beyond talking, and to move philosophical ideas of peace from their minds into their bodies.

I'll never forget one evening after an *aiki* session in a village near Nablus, when a group of 25 Palestinian activists who had been detained and jailed asked:

"How do you think we might approach our national liberation struggle using aikido ideas?"

We talked for hours into the night, considering this amazing question. How humbling it was to feel aikido's power in capturing the imagination of even militants as a viable alternative to violence, and freshly energizing their efforts for peace and justice.

2003-2005 - Aiki Extensions founder, Don Levine, had been working to do something '*aiki*' in the Middle East, and phoned to ask about my experiences there. I told him how since the Oslo accords, I had dreamed of doing a 'Salaam Shalom' aikido event or even of establishing a *dojo* with both Palestinians and Israelis. That Arabic-Hebrew phrase helped fire up AE's watershed *Training Across Borders* conference held in Cyprus in 2005, and the establishment of the ongoing *Middle East Aikido Project*. MAP has since partnered with *Budo For Peace* in Israel; spawned the *Peace Camp Initiative, Aikido Without Borders*, and the *Awassa Youth Dojo* in Ethiopia; connected with *aikidoka* in Jordan and war-torn Iraq; and helped nurture the first generation of Palestinian practitioners and black belts, both inside of Israel and at the central *dojo* now growing in the West Bank capital city of Ramallah.

Cyprus seemed full of life-changing moments every minute. One hundred people raised in hatred for one another; Arabs and Jews, Serbs and Bosnians, Turks and Greeks, all took the courageous step to meet in a neutral land because of their common love of and belief in aikido.

A Way to Reconcile the World

Real-world enemies meditated, stretched, and even exchanged massages in early morning sessions. In addition to technique training on the mat, optional workshops were held to explore *aiki*-based leadership, healing from trauma, and youth training programs in poverty-stricken and violent areas. Everyone came to every session! There were people from all sorts of troubled areas geographically, all together enjoying African tribal dancing, universal Beatle's choruses, and a wild and wonderful cross-cultural talent show highlighted by an Iraqi's hilarious impersonation of Saddam Hussein.

I'll never forget being moved to my core when one Jordanian complained:

"Aikido is making our life so hard! We liked to hate, and now we can't!"

The following quotes really say it all, about aikido and what is possible when diverse people gather together to practice:

"Aikido lets us share harmonizing our movements. This is so needed! That way we can come closer and combine the actual people that represent the different sides. I wish to plant peace by doing peace." *Dekel, Israel*

"It's an unbelievable feeling to see the things in people's eyes here." *Caner, Turkey*

"A lifetime experience. From this moment, the world is my family." *Spiros, Greece*

"Amazing. Heaven on Earth for four days. We managed to pull off what governments only dream about." *Scott, Turkey*

"It was great to meet aikidoists from all over the world, especially countries I am not yet allowed to visit." *Efrat, Israel.*

"These days were a good reminder to an easily forgotten fact. We are all people. Thank you for the opportunity to raise my eyes from the narrow sight of daily stressful life, and realize there is a bigger and much more beautiful picture to see." *Eyal, Israel.*

"This seminar achieved its goals, and went far beyond. We proved that the training mat is a perfect tool that helps people forget their hate, and even love each other. I hope the seeds of peace planted in Cyprus will grow very quickly, and that we will be able to see their positive impacts on our reality." *Khaled, Palestine.*

"I put myself in the hands of O Sensei second and God first, decided to jump… and landed in a bed of roses too good to be true. There was a harmony and energy flow unlike I ever experienced and it split my heart in two."-*Alaa, Jordan*

"Glow, peace, glow." *Ayman, Jordan*

Several years later, one teenage girl, a Bedouin Martial Artist For Peace from Israel, wrote in her application for our Aiki Extensions Peace Camp Initiative program:

"My big idea is to start with the little children."

And as it says on the Peace Pole which serves as O Sensei's headstone in Tanabe, Japan:

"May Peace Prevail On Earth"!

Vancouver 2012. - Aikido's inherent power to effect greater inner peace, health and success never ceases to be a fountain of inspiration. In a meditation some years ago, the phrase came that 'people of power and influence' need this training. So I started extending my work into *aiki* and somatic-based peak performance trainings for corporate and conference groups, frequently ending with this true story.

Some 500 people from around the San Francisco Bay area filled the Aikido West *dojo* for a *dan* grading one Sunday. This was in the 1980s and Wendy Palmer was holding her, and Richard Strozzi-Heckler's, infant son in her arms. Saotome *Sensei* was there and decided to do a multiple sword attack demonstration that O Sensei used to do. He called for about a dozen black belts to encircle him with *bokken* in hand. But before starting the demo, he came over to say "Hi" to Wendy and to meet their new son.

Whereupon he took the baby in his arms and then walked into the center of the circle.

With a spirited "*HAJIME*!" the black belts all attacked, full force. Saotome *Sensei* slipped off the line and cheerfully began skipping around the *dojo*, eluding every strike, holding the baby with one arm and occasionally using the other to throw or disarm an attacker. Everyone else sat watching nervously, riveted, hardly breathing. When "*YAME*!" was called, Sensei came back over to Wendy and wished her sweet son well in life.

While the whole demonstration was stunning, perhaps most amazing was that the baby never fussed or cried. I happened to be standing next to Wendy, and felt incredulous as *Sensei* returned the infant to his mother. The tiny guy was as quiet and serene as when he had left, a few super-intense scary minutes before!

This experience, filled with so many aikido lessons for life, has become a powerful teaching story. It was a brilliant demonstration of the ability to remain calm and clear under pressure. Staying centered instead of succumbing to stress. Not reacting to, but moving skilfully with and mastering the energies of opposition, chaos and fear that might otherwise cause harm or defeat. Once when I asked a group of business executives how the baby stayed so calm, one man was moved to tears as he said:

"It was the sensei's energy. He stayed calm inside, which the baby felt and so he was able to stay okay. I just got it. I'm the CEO of my company and I need to be sensei! How I am matters, inside and out. What I do with my energy makes all the difference. My employees are my babies. So are my wife and kids. EVERYONE is really."

Late 1990's-2013 - My dear mother Esther ('Essie') left the earth after a long, brave struggle with Alzheimer's. The disease came like a relentless thief, stealing more and more of her memory, cognition and abilities. But incredibly, while her body and brain shrank, even Alzheimer's could not touch her heart or spirit. At Mom's graveside service my sister said:

"Despite her inevitable decline, Essie was able to maintain her core being, spreading her goodness and love and signature smile wherever she went. Although she had become heart-breakingly vulnerable, her compassionate, feisty, beautiful self prevailed. And we were all in her thrall."

A Way to Reconcile the World

As awful and destructive as the dementia was, I've often wondered what allowed Mom to remain so radiant and brilliant. Not because I am partial to aikido, but I really feel that the secret ingredients lie in *ai/love* and *ki/*life-energy.

We made it our family's business to figure out how to best be with Essie, so that she could enjoy the highest possible quality of life that she was capable of, at every step and turn along the way. The crucial key turned out to be in what is commonly referred to as 'going with the flow,' from an inner place of acceptance. It is the *ai* in aikido: loving, harmonizing, and blending with what is.

At first, as memory deficits and personality changes started to manifest in Mom's behaviors, we would become impatient or critical or forceful. She would say and do things that seemed silly or crazy or just too inexplicable or sad for anyone to know how to deal with them. We would react in our usual ways using logic, or persuasion, or even censure, only to discover that we weren't getting through and were in fact adding to a distress that we couldn't begin to fathom.

So we began to read a lot, studied and worked on our own counterproductive responses. When Mom would say or do odd things, we stopped reacting oddly or trying to correct her. When she got frustrated or obstinate, we learned to give more understanding. Harshness had to go. We stopped resisting her resistance, and stopped insisting that she be less insistent. She was desperately losing control of her mind and life, so every sense of control she could retain was important.

We started looking out past the pain of things she couldn't do, to find things she could do. Down to small things, like helping fold a towel or sheet, or placing a dish in the dishwasher. And whether she did the tiniest task well or not didn't matter at all. It was just time to enjoy being together, and for her to be able and valu-able. With our delight in her, she seemed to become ever more delightful, whereas our upset at her had only caused more upset that nobody enjoyed.

Instead of arguing with Mom, we learned to agree and go along in ways that made her feel good, and that prevented crisis from developing. Talk about off-the-mat aikido practice! Our hearts broke open with even more love as Essie somehow devolved/evolved into an indescribable love and sweetness that melted all our moments with her.

The 'Essence of Essie' was truly her loving life-energy. Above all she demonstrated that even when cognition fails, people can maintain vital *ki* and knowingness, and are fuelled by *ai*. We often hear that we are not our bodies or minds but what might be called 'spirit' or soul: a non-material but very real life-force that animates the body and mind. We are all sacred beings attuned with emotional and energetic intelligence. Love, from within and around us, is needed so we can live and flourish. Even when Mom didn't know our names, or her way around the house, or how to use a fork or toothbrush, her spirit resonated to love and kept her strong and aware.

Essie's *ki* never waned and was clearly indestructible, even through her dying moments. I was sitting beside her bed, just as the hospice nurse and the rest of the family had left the room. She took that opportunity to slip out of her body, without even a last breath to warn me. Frantic, I called everyone. I think Mom, who had become pure spirit before my very eyes, knew that we weren't ok with her leaving like that, because *she came back*!

Before all our eyes, with two giant loud breaths, we watched as she re-entered her body! With great love and extra-ordinary presence, she started breathing again. She stayed with us for 36 more unbelievable minutes. And then she dissolved once again into formless spirit as she sublimely departed from this physical plane. It was so clear that only her body had died, while her essential *ki* was alive and well and moving right along to greater realms beyond.

While Mom's disease and dying moments were so intimate, it seems important to share her stories. *Ai* and *ki* in utmost action. I can only bow to Essie and the universe - and to everyone really - and follow the Way of these ultimate lessons of life-energy and of love.

The Body Might Not Be Willing, But the Mind Is Strong
by
Judith Jones - KSMBDA - England - 1st Dan

I was diagnosed with rheumatoid arthritis in 1988 when I was 18 years old. At that time I spent many months in too much pain to get out of bed. I was given some drugs that helped bring the arthritis under control for a while and some months later I started practising aikido. When I started training, my muscles were still very weak from having spent so much time not moving. I found that by extending *ki*, and channelling the other person's movements I could still successfully practise aikido, even with wasted muscles.

Many of the exercises were painful, but I enjoyed the practice immensely and it helped my muscles to grow strong again. I loved it, particularly the philosophy behind it which included the concepts of non-violence and calmness. I also liked the fact that we were all working together, to help improve each other's skills rather than competing. As Wasyl Kolesnikov, (my teacher) said,

"It's not one-upmanship, it's all upmanship."

I met many kind and generous people through aikido who are good friends of mine to this day, and working with them I earned my black belt in 1996.

The skills I learnt on the mat, also helped me in my working life. Particularly when teaching maths, English and science to troubled and sometimes violent children who had been expelled from school.

Some of the young people I worked with had drug problems. I found the skills I had learnt on the mat were invaluable. It was important when working with these children to stay calm and to focus on the positive in any situation. Many of these young people came to trust me. They understood that I had their best interests at heart, and a good few gained excellent exam results, with me as their only teacher for all their subjects. One girl who had spent some time in a young offenders institution before

I met her, managed to stay out of trouble and went on to sixth form college for further study.

In terms of my practice on the mat, unfortunately the effects of my rheumatoid arthritis became increasingly severe, which meant that I could practice less and less often and ultimately I had to stop.

My practice off the mat, however, has never stopped. Since 2008, I have been unable to work, and rarely able to leave my house. I am in continual pain, but the skills and mental attitudes I learned on the mat help me deal with whatever life throws at me.

I am positive and happy despite my problems. I keep moving and I'm not giving up. I still do what I can to support my fellow human beings. I can take the time to listen to people and offer support, on the phone or over the Internet, even though I am stuck in my house.

Timing
by
Linda Holiday - Aikido of Santa Cruz - U.S.A. - 6th Dan

I was driving into town behind a pickup truck whose driver had evidently just made a purchase at the lumber yard. A stack of long boards, roped together, rested in the bed of the truck and extended well beyond the roof of the cab. The boards looked to be about a foot wide.

I followed the pickup up a steep grade. Another pickup truck zoomed up behind and began to tailgate me. As the road levelled off and we all gathered speed, I watched the top board stir in the breeze, nudging the rope holding it down. The pickup behind me was still tailgating me, and I kept careful watch in my rear view mirror. A sense of discomfort grew and persisted.

Finally I yielded to intuition. I slowed way down and pulled over into a driveway to let the second pickup pass me. At that moment I heard a loud "crack!" and saw the top board break off in the wind. It spun through the air and crashed on the spot on the road where I would have been.

The timing had been perfect. If I had pulled over any earlier, the tailgating pickup would have rushed up behind the other truck and been in just the right position to be hit by the flying board. Not only had I escaped from harm myself, but the driver of the truck following me had been protected as well.

気　気　気

Practising Ukemi
by
Simon Collier - Iwada Ryu Osaka - Japan - 3rd Dan

I came to Japan to study aikido intensively 13 years ago. After I arrived, I found a *dojo* that could sponsor me for a cultural visa. I then spent the next two years training five or six days a week. *Ukemi* was always my weak point, but I gradually became competent enough. I trained hard and earned *shodan* but never had to use techniques outside of the *dojo* apart from *irimi* when moving through crowded Osaka stations and bars.

Eventually my work became too busy and I essentially had to stop practicing for a while. Then one day as I was walking along a street talking with a friend and not looking where I was going, I walked into a row of bicycles. As the bicycles and I started to fall over, my *ukemi* training kicked in. I sailed smoothly over the bicycles and then rather than crashing into the concrete I effortlessly rolled and came up walking. This was definitely the best *ukemi* I had ever done.

My friend's reaction was something like "Sasuga Simon", meaning 'Trust Simon'. I did, and still do, have the reputation of being more than a little clumsy. She didn't actually see the *ukemi* properly, she just saw the result. When everyone else realized what had happened though, they followed by saying, 'Sugoi, sugoi, sugoi" (great, great, great).

Since then, after a long period as *ronin*, I've changed *dojo* and now assist my teacher, I hope to take my *sandan* test later this year.

In regard to that *ukemi* it always reminds me that when something comes naturally to us we can smoothly overcome obstacles that block our path without panic or anger.

It reminds me to train harder.

Editor's note - *Since writing this story, Simon has indeed achieved sandan.*

Control the Head and You Control the Body
by
Brad Manosevitz - Aikido Aspen - U.S.A. - 3rd Dan

At one time, I was managing the security team at a local bar and restaurant, 'The Seabright Brewery'. Usually, it was a pretty chill place but certain nights of the week were very busy, so we needed people at the door to check IDs and make sure things stayed within bounds.

By now, I had worked the door enough to know that if someone came in and I sensed they might be trouble later, eight times out of 10, they would be. On one of the busy nights that I was working, there was a large table of guys who were kind of rowdy and loud. I stopped over to say hello and to let them know that we expected them to behave and that they could stay as long as they did so.

Nevertheless, it wasn't long before they were verbally abusing one of the waitresses. I went over and asked them to leave. I had also done this job long enough to know that throwing out one person was something you never do alone. So, I went over with a few of my team to encourage these guys out. As expected, their reaction to our request was a negative one and as they got up, they started to make a fuss.

As one guy was leaving, he picked up a chair and threw it at no one in particular. Fortunately it didn't hit any of the other guests.

I was walking directly behind one of the others in this group as he made his way to the door. Suddenly, he made a move as though he wanted to head back into the bar. Being close to him, I very lightly put my hands along his jaw line on both sides of his head. It was the same kind of move that one might expect to learn in a CPR or first aid class, when one is required to stabilize the head and neck. With his head between my gentle hands, and my hands moving in front of me in the direction of the door, the rest of his body had no choice but to follow. It took very little effort for me to continue to move him. Once out the door, I released him. No need for further action. Mission accomplished.

Control the head, and you will likely control the rest of the body. Pay attention to your intuition. If something doesn't feel right, it probably isn't.

気 気 気

I Heard My Instructor's Voice
by

Jesse Solis - Aikido of Santa Cruz (formerly North Bay Aikido) - U.S.A.

One Sunday evening I had taken my father home and was closing up his workplace, a gas station and small store on the corner of a highway about a mile outside of Salinas. As I was heading out of the store to take the final readings from the gas pumps, I saw a car go around the corner with several men in it. The way they looked at me gave me a strange, nervous feeling. Then they disappeared around the corner. In response to the apprehension I felt, I took the precaution of locking the store and turning off the store lights before I went out to the pumps. My car was parked between the store and one set of pumps.

While taking the pump readings, I suddenly heard a car door slam. It was same car I had seen before, and two men got out of it. One of them asked me if he could use the phone in the store. I pointed out a pay phone a hundred yards away. Then he asked if he could buy a quart of oil. I told him the store was closed. Still they lingered. Then he asked if he could borrow a dime. I fished through my pockets and found no change, so I went to my car to look there.

As I sat in the driver's seat of my car, one foot on the pavement, fishing through the ashtray for loose change, one man was standing behind the open car door, the other man in front by the hood. The man by the car door was short and slight and wore a long overcoat. The other man was about six feet tall and weighed maybe 250 pounds. The first guy told me to get in their car. I heard him but ignored what he said. I knew that something was wrong, and I was trying hard to act natural and unconcerned.

"Get in the car," he repeated.

I stayed where I was and said simply, "Here's your dime."

The man looked very angry. He began to raise a long object out from under his overcoat. It snagged on his coat as he fumbled with it. Instinctively, I jumped out of my car and grabbed the object from the side with both hands. It was the barrel of a shotgun! Suddenly I became conscious of the potential danger from the other guy who was now behind me. As I hesitated, the first man stepped back, and the shotgun slid out from between my hands. He levelled the shotgun at my chest. I stepped back, raised my hands in the air, and closed my eyes.

"I hope this won't hurt too much," I thought.

After a couple of heartbeats I opened my eyes. I was still alive. I was feeling weary and hopeless. I just did not want to be there at all. I felt myself drifting away, as if I had left my body and was looking at the scene from some other place. I had been training at Aikido of Monterey for about two years. Inside my head, I heard the voice of my instructor, Danielle Smith, saying,

"Stay centered. Stay calm."

With a tremendous effort I pulled myself back together to face my situation.

I was trapped between the two men, the car and the gas pump island. At that moment, the big man behind me grabbed me from behind. He wrapped his huge arm around my shoulders, drawing it up towards my neck in a chokehold. At first I was drawn off balance, backwards and up on my toes. Then I remembered my aikido training, and I felt as if I were on the mat, practicing a *kubishime* choke. I heard my instructor's voice coaching me encouragingly. I stepped back towards the man, regaining my balance by moving into his grip. I remembered to hook my hand around his choking arm and lock my own arm against my chest. I could feel him straining to put the choke on, but I stayed relaxed and grounded, and although I offered him no resistance, he was not able to choke me.

Then I felt the sharp prick of a knifepoint at the back of my neck. I moved even closer to the man, molding my body into his, so I could feel his every movement. I relaxed completely and waited, praying for an opening to present itself.

"Where's the money?" he hissed into my ear.

"What money?" I stalled, momentarily confusing him.

The smaller man, who was still aiming the gun at me, repeated,

"Where's the money?"

"There is no money," I said, "My father took it."

"Took it where?" he persisted.

"Home," I answered.

This was not true. What money there was hidden in the store, but I wanted to preserve my options. Also, we had been robbed before. We just couldn't afford to lose more money.

The man with the gun appeared frustrated and perplexed and began to look around. The big man choking me relaxed his grip for a split-second there was my opening! I spun out of his grasp in a *tenkan* turn. I stood by the gas pumps where I was no longer in between the men and I could keep both of them in my field of vision. I saw the big man's face contort in anger at my escape. He raised the knife in order to step forward and stab me.

Instinctively, before he had time to take a step, I shifted into a *hanmi* stance and extended both arms and my center towards him in a classic aikido extension. I felt my whole spirit projecting towards him. I was amazed to see him fade back as if he had been knocked backwards by a powerful blow. Now there was a buffer of space between us. Quickly, I turned toward the gunman; I looked at him calmly with my hands up and open. The gunman asked for my wallet and I gave it to him with no hesitation. I thought that maybe they would leave now.

"Get in the car!" the gunman suddenly ordered.

Terror filled me again. I remembered the Salinas River less than a mile away, and all the dead bodies that had been found in it over the years.

"NO!" I said, "No, I won't go with you."

It was a genuine and powerful refusal, powered by my will to live. I recognized this feeling. I had seen women empowered in self-defense classes say "NO!" with just that same authority. I slipped out between the gas pumps and began to sidle out behind the island.

The small man confronted me, the shotgun still aimed at my chest.

"Where are you going?" he demanded.

"Nowhere," I assured him, making eye contact with him, "I'm right here."

The other man's attention seemed to have wandered. He was leaning against a gas pump, his chin propped in his hand as if he were idly watching traffic. Then he spoke up.

"Just shoot the fucker! Shoot him!"

I knew I had to maintain a connection with the gunman or he just might do what his friend said. I said to him,

"Look, I won't go with you, but take the car. It's yours. The keys are in the car. Just take it!"

He appeared to think it over for a moment, and then he suddenly jumped into the driver's seat of my car. I saw my opening and I took off across the fields to my neighbour's house, where I called the police, with the keys to my car safely in my pocket.

気　気　気

Taking a Stance
by
Kayla Feder, - Aikido of Berkeley - U.S.A. - 6th Dan

Aikido has been my life since the age of 10. So it's difficult to choose my most memorable aikido experience, since aikido has brought so much richness and beauty into my life.

As many *aikidoka* would agree, the training that we do on the mat changes the way we relate to our whole lives, and especially to the way we deal with confrontation. I have been attacked verbally and physically, and each time it has felt to me as if there were a specific aspect of aikido that I was being shown, but most of all I learned that it worked.

However, one particular story does stand out in my mind. For a number of years, I lived in what was considered a dangerous neighbourhood in Oakland. I had a dog that was part Labrador and part Pit Bull; his name was Jasper. Jasper and I would take runs in my neighbourhood. On one of our runs, a man blocked the side walk and told me that I had to give Jasper to him or he would hurt both of us. Without thinking, I immediately went into *hanmi*, bent my knees and stood firm and grounded, while looking the man directly in the eye. Amazingly, I did not feel afraid, maintaining my stance only a few feet away from this large man who had threatened to hurt me if I didn't give him my cherished Jasper. I felt enveloped by compassion, and so my gaze only expressed compassion.

In that moment, there was a meeting of minds and he felt it too. He lowered his fist and walked away. As he walked away, I knew that I had just done a perfect aikido technique. I was firm in my *hanmi*, which expressed the yang or positive part of the technique, at the same time I felt completely compassionate toward my aggressor, which expressed the yin aspect or receptive part of the technique.

The amazing thing was that I had just been teaching these aspects in class and suddenly here was the opportunity to experience the reality and to feel the effectiveness of the spirit of aikido.

気　気　気

Aikido, Cerebral Palsy and Daily Life
by
Chance Gorman - Aikido Aberdeen Yuishinkai - Scotland - 7th Kyu

I have hemiplegic cerebral palsy, a neuro-muscular condition affecting the spatial-motor abilities of my left side. I was born three months and two weeks premature, weighing one pound six ounces. My entire body could fit inside the palm of an average adult's hand. The Lord preserved me from dying innumerable times.

As a severely premature infant, I suffered three intraventricular hemorrhages (IVHs). The following is a brief explanation of an IVH. The human brain floats in a liquid called cerebral spinal fluid. Encasing that fluid is a network of blood ventricles that supports and protects the brain. As one would imagine, the pressure exerted by the cerebral-spinal fluid is far less than that exerted by one's blood pressure.

Many highly premature infants experience a hemorrhage of one or more blood vessels. Burst vessels can send blood shooting out into the brain and destroy collections of nerve cells or 'bundles.' The results are frequently fatal or greatly damaging to one's mental and physical development.

As mentioned above, I suffered three such hemorrhages. The IVHs destroyed nerve bundles within my motor cortex, the center of the brain responsible for voluntary movement. Neurophysiology dictates the right side of the motor cortex controls the left side of the body and the left side of the motor cortex controls the right side of the body. Nerve bundles within the right side of my motor cortex were destroyed. Thus, such damage affected the entirety of my left side and resulted in hemiplegic cerebral palsy.

Cerebral palsy may be classified (simplistically) by its three primary neuro-muscular manifestations:

1. *Spasticity* - This form is characterized by severe muscular tightness and rigidity. One may visualize the effects of this by thinking of a bicep muscle in a constantly flexed state without being able to relax the muscle.
2. *Flaccidity* - This is the inability to flex, tighten, or contract one's muscle(s) at will.
3. *A combination of spasticity and flaccidity* - Such a state is where certain muscles of the body are in a constant state of tightness, while others are unable to tighten or flex.

I have the third category throughout my left side. As such, my left arm and leg are significantly weaker than my right arm and leg. I also have to wear an orthotic (brace) on my left leg to facilitate proper ambulatory function.

My balance is also greatly affected by the cerebral palsy. Functioning, walking, and running with the condition is analogous to conducting all matters of one's life (particularly walking and running) on a balance beam.

Cerebral palsy also impairs one's proprioception. Proprioception may be termed "the mind's eye" or that physiological instrument whereby the mind perceives and represents the body to itself as a unified and inter-connected whole. My proprioceptive abilities were significantly damaged by virtue of the IVHs.

I underwent much physical therapy to build up awareness and usage of the muscles. Nevertheless, my parents consistently had to remind me to use my left side in performing daily activities. An example will illustrate what I mean. I would attempt to make my bed before I went to school. I would do this only using one arm. My father or mother would enter the room and have to remind me to "use both hands." Then, I would begin to make my bed using both arms and hands.

I would often tell people who wanted to understand these issues that I 'forget' my left arm/side, but, in truth, that is simply not the case. I always know it is there, rather, it does not enter my mind to use my left arm/side, when it would be beneficial to do so.

My abilities increased and my proprioceptive issues lessened over the years. Nevertheless, cerebral palsy continues to influence my daily living skills and functions greatly.

I started aikido nearly six months prior to this writing. As one trains barefoot, I had to forego the use of my orthotic. It has been challenging, but I have really enjoyed and still enjoy practicing aikido. I train four times per week.

Several weeks after I started, my orthotic broke and I had no immediate replacement. For the eight months prior to this, I had been doing a great deal of jogging in an effort to strengthen my leg and now I was diligently doing my aikido training. After several days without my brace, I noticed my left leg functioned more like the right leg, than ever before. I was ecstatic. I also noticed increased proprioceptive abilities. For example, my right hand would be busy and, instead of ceasing whatever I was doing with my right hand to attend to another matter, I simply (and rather naturally) would use my left hand to perform the task.

It is now possible that with intense training and a good deal of determination I could walk normally with minimal or no use of my orthotic, though it might take a few years.

My left arm and hand are also increasing in strength. The Lord Jesus is good. I look forward to continuing my training and progressively improving the motor use of my left arm, hand and leg.

Aikido has been and is a true blessing throughout my daily life.

気 気 気

On Not Creating an Enemy

by

David Sofen - Aikido of Santa Cruz - U.S.A. - 4th Dan

I was in a doctors' meeting in which we were discussing policy on a controversial issue. The group seemed divided and we had yet to reach a common ground. Being one of the younger physicians, I had saved my opinion for the tail end of the discussion. I argued my point calmly, but forcefully, as it was over an issue that had major implications for a patient's civil rights. My opinion was completely opposite to the chair of the meeting, the medical director of the clinic, and my boss. As I finished talking, he exploded in a rage, turning red as he blasted my opinion and re-argued his.

I realized I wasn't breathing. I was training for a *kyu* exam at the time, so I took some deep breaths and began thinking of the various techniques I knew. None seemed appropriate for verbal warfare. As he yelled on, I began to wonder if my job were at stake. I knew I had to do something. I remembered a story from class about not creating an enemy. I realized that because he was yelling at me, I had assumed that he was my enemy. *Irimi* popped into my head. I realized I needed to enter.

As he finished his yelling and the meeting broke up, I kept breathing. I walked up to him, smiled, batted my eyes, touched him on the shoulder and said,

"Gee, I hope 1 didn't upset you with what I said."

For an instant he was stunned, and then, blushing and laughing, he apologized for getting so vehement. I pushed on,

"Well, you know, for a minute there I thought you were angry at me."

"Oh no, no; I always get excited when discussing topics like this. In fact, this was nothing. You should see when I really get angry."

I thought to myself that I had no desire to see him really angry, but I just smiled and said nothing. As we walked back to the clinic, he put his arm on my shoulder and commended me on the work I was doing. To this day we are on friendly terms and we have agreed to disagree on this one subject.

気 気 気

Aiki Impact on My Life
by
Robert Hill - Trowbridge Aikikai - England - 6th Dan

Students of aikido will always ask the following questions:

"Does aikido work?"

"Sensei, have you ever used aikido?"

"What is aikido?"

When I began aikido, I remember another student who had been to a few classes. He made some extra money selling ice cream out of a van. One morning, he came to practice in a very excited state and told us all how he had applied *nikyo* to someone who had tried to steal his takings. When I was young that was what I wanted to hear; it answered all my questions.

Recently, I read 'Thinking, Fast and Slow' by Daniel Kahneman, which seeks to explain how when we perceive things, we order them into patterns, and how we make decisions about what to do as a result. The book looks at and seeks to explain the phenomenon of expert intuition, and gives examples, such as the legendary deductive powers possessed by Sherlock Holmes and Roger Federer, who always seems to anticipate where his opponent will hit the ball. Kahneman shows that this is not some magical ability, but a direct result of having done the proverbial 10,000 hours of practice.

Reading the book brought to mind and explained for me several instances of intuitive responses in my own life, which showed me that the practice of aikido extends itself into daily life in useful, practical and surprising ways. The following simple tales illustrate that my practice has become embedded in my daily life and answers those common questions about aikido in a much more meaningful way.

I attended an aikido training camping at the Abbaye de Maredsous, which is situated in the Meuse River Valley, Belgium, for two or three days of inner aikido with the late Seiichi Sugano Shihan. A group of us were taking a walk in the sun after morning practice and lunch. We were relaxed, fit, and calm and enjoying strolling down an avenue of tall trees, while swapping stories and eating ice cream. Just then, I noticed a woman's small handkerchief on the ground. Nothing unusual there. Maredsous is a famous tourist area and many members of the local bourgeoisie take the drive up into the hills to eat at the restaurant, to buy produce made by the monks, and to exercise their small dogs. We kept walking. I looked ahead.

Fifty metres away, I saw a well-dressed, elderly woman looking a bit distressed, searching for something in her handbag and then on the ground around her. Without thinking, I spun on my heels, went back and picked up the handkerchief. I returned to the group, who had barely noted my detour. We carried on walking. When we got closer to the woman I held out the handkerchief and said, "Madam?"

"Oh! Merci beaucoup, Monsieur," she said gratefully as she reclaimed the white handkerchief.

Whilst backpacking in India in late 1977, I was walking along a Calcutta street, one part of a bustling river of humanity. I made brief eye contact with a young man three or four yards ahead of me, coming in my direction. The next thing I knew there was an elbow in my face. I dodged out of the way and was about to continue my walk, when instinctively my hand went to my breast pocket, where I had been carrying a gold-coloured pen. It was gone. I pivoted and the young man was standing behind me, within perfect striking distance. The guy froze on the spot. I put out my hand and said,

"Give it back!"

He hesitated for a little while, then he reached into his pocket, took out my pen and put it in my hand. He paused for a moment longer, before quickly turning, finding a gap in the moving crowd and then running off.

In 2008, I was on holiday with my family in Turkey. It was a very hot day in the Mediterranean sun. We had been walking around all morning and sat down on a bench in a small square to enjoy the shade of a tree and have a drink. Across the square was a man who was obviously intoxicated or perhaps mentally disturbed. He was rifling through a collection of food containers and brown paper bags in what seemed like his personal section of the square. He was shouting out and approaching people who came near him. We were out of his range and when he came near we turned away to avoid further engagement. As more and more people chose to avoid him, he began wandering around the square, shouting and peering at people. He wasn't a real threat, but it was uncomfortable for those around him.

Despite doing what we could to ignore him, he approached us, speaking Turkish and gesturing that he wanted food. We had none; so I offered him some water, but he didn't want that. We could only gesture that we had nothing else to give him. He wandered away, but quickly returned and made straight for my partner, who now looked quite alarmed. She moved away from him, but he kept getting closer and closer, speaking louder and louder.

I was beginning to feel the effects of adrenalin kicking in, fight or flight. He reached out to grab my partner. From somewhere I let out a *kiai* shout that would have knocked birds out of the sky. I felt everyone in the square stop to look and see what was going on. By now I was on my feet and going for the guy. He went strangely limp, looked around as though he had suddenly wakened from a stupor and then he wandered off, as if nothing had happened. Minutes later he was approaching other people just as before, but he did keep looking back at me to check where I was.

Working as a high school teacher in Australia, 25 or so years ago, I had to discipline a lad about something or other. I knew that this boy practiced either karate or taekwondo. Indeed it was one thing we had in common, and it was exactly the sort of thing teachers look for in order to make even fragile contact with angry kids.

As I was talking firmly to this boy, he adopted all of the characteristic defensive tricks. He hunched his shoulders, turned his head away, replied in mumbled monosyllables and refused to make eye contact. All I could feel was anger boiling inside him. At one very specific moment, he looked directly into my eyes. I realised straight away that I was within kicking range and that the lad was making very quick decisions. Could he? Should he?

Before he could decide I moved my body just out of range. He dropped his eyes again. With that subtle change of relationship, I chose to change tactics and refrained from further interrogation. From that point on, we were able to resolve the situation.

Through aikido I have learned about myself. Primarily, I have become happy knowing that I do not have anything to prove. From this perspective, I realise that there is time to perceive more of what is going on around me. Fewer things happen to me. I see more things coming before they arrive. There is time to get out of the way, if I want. There is a choice. One begins to think that perhaps one is doing aikido all the time, just sometimes there is awareness and sometimes there is not.

To end with another tale: When I worked for Ford in Dagenham during the late 1970s, I used to catch a train from Barking to get to the plant. Hundreds of guys would be on the platform each morning waiting for the train. Some days it was very noisy; some days it was eerily quiet with thick fog. Every morning though, a good while before our train could be heard or seen, one particular man would suddenly get up from his seat and walk to the platform edge and within a short time the train would arrive. I found out later he was blind.

Finding a Connection
by
M-J Marvesley - Aberdeen Aikido Yuishinkai - Scotland - 1st Kyu

I have been involved with aikido for more than six years now. It impacts on most aspects of my life particularly my work and how I relate to others. As a result, it is becoming increasingly important to me. I work as a support practitioner for people with learning disabilities and often I am alone, working out in the community with no immediate colleagues to turn to for advice when things get difficult. I often need to react fast and adapt to whatever is going on with my clients.

Frequently, I support individuals who demonstrate challenging behaviour. At the beginning of this stage in my career, this could be very difficult, as I had faced nothing like it before. I did not have a background in the care sector and the training with my company was quite basic. At the start, I was not confident when I met new people, let alone those who could be aggressive and demanding. It was daunting and I had to keep reminding myself that I could face most situations. Training in aikido taught me that if I show confidence outwardly (even if I might not necessarily feel confident within) and project a positive attitude, then difficult situations can be easily dealt with.

The responses of some of my clients can often make it very difficult for them to participate in daily tasks and they can struggle to integrate into the community. When faced with the everyday situations that most of us perceive as normal, my clients can become nervous and stressed, expressing this through the only way they know how – challenging behaviour.

When I first started the job, I worked closely with a client who would often be quite aggressive towards staff. Initially, when I met her, I was intimidated. She was a lot bigger than me and if she wanted to, she could swat me away like a fly. She showed her aggression in many different ways, but mainly she would hit surfaces. This would make a loud bang and made her seem terrifying.

There were a number of things that might trigger this, such as; not wanting to participate in a task, feeling frustrated, becoming anxious, or when she was over-tired, to name a few. This meant that she would often miss out on participation in activities with staff, both in her home and in the local community. I did not feel comfortable taking her out for a coffee, fearing that she might become aggressive with me or with those around us. This seemed very unfair on her, as it meant that she received few opportunities to integrate into the local community and she was not being given any strategies that would help her to deal with the situations that she found so difficult.

My first encounter with her was very stressful, and within the first 10 minutes of supporting her, I had to withdraw from her house. This was the first time I had to deal with something like this and I did not know how to handle it. I feared for my own safety and could not see anything other than how it was affecting me. I didn't understand that she was stressed by meeting a new member of staff. Withdrawing as I did was a mistake because she now believed that she could scare me away easily, if she wanted to.

As weeks went by, I began to learn more about her. I began to accept her for what she was, despite her aggression. When she showed signs of this, shouting, hitting walls and so forth, I would stand calmly in the same area and wait for it to pass. I noticed quite quickly that despite all the drama, she would never touch staff (well, very rarely), and it was more a case of giving her the space to vent her emotion in a supportive, non-judgemental way.

Through my experience with aikido, I found that I was better placed than my colleagues when faced with the potential threat of a physical attack. I was able to remain calm and I was better equipped to see whether the threat of a physical attack was coming, or whether this lady was simply venting her frustration on nearby walls. This calm approach led to her outbursts becoming less frequent and lasting for shorter periods of time. She began to realise that I understood and accepted her. She could behave any way she felt she needed to and I would stand by her and support her to deal with her emotions.

I realised that often she was looking for a reaction from staff members. This would lead to conflict, which she didn't know how to end and which meant that her support was over before she had had the benefit of it. But when things kicked off with me, I remained calm (and poured forth positive *ki*). This positivity rubbed off on her, allowing her an escape route and a way of ending any possible conflicts she saw arising. I discussed this calm approach with colleagues, including my team leader, who also began to accept this aspect of her character. They too experimented with remaining calm in the face of her aggression.

After almost a year of working with this individual, there has been a marked improvement in her life. She very seldom behaves as she did, and if she does it is usually because she is faced with a new situation or with unfamiliar staff, who haven't been taught how to work with her. She has begun to talk to me, explaining when she is upset or frustrated rather than shouting or being physical.

She has learnt that this gets the same non-judgemental response and so she has a choice as to how she deals with things. It is wonderful to see how her life has benefited from this calm approach. She is now a valued member of her community and able to go do her shopping alone, where she often makes friends with shop assistants.

She goes to the cinema, takes herself off to have a coffee, and very recently she has started to push herself into situations that she previously would have found hugely stressful, such as shopping in crowded areas. She is proud of herself and a more confident, calm individual.

There has also been a marked change in the team that works with her and in its work with other individuals. They have gained a new confidence to stand their ground and remain calm in stressful situations, which has a positive impact on the people we work with as well as on the team as a whole.

I didn't start aikido with these sorts of benefits in mind, but then perhaps, I didn't truly understand what it was all about.

気 気 気

Raw Meat in the Lion's Den
by
Gary Hughes - Aboyne Aikido Club - Scotland - 4th Kyu

Every student teacher remembers his or her first lesson. Standing on your own, in front of up to 30 potentially hostile pupils who are watching your every move and waiting for any error or weakness that they can exploit for a few moments of fun. Now imagine that your first lesson is with a class filled with 15-year-olds. They look to pounce upon any fresh meat that has been thrown into a lions' den.

When I was faced with this, I entered the room calmly with a relaxed and open posture. No fiddling, twitching, or hiding. I stood in front of the class and introduced myself, just like the bow in the *dojo* before *randori*. I started the lesson with questions, my goal being to assess their current level of knowledge. In reality, it was more about me staying in control of the situation.

It started off well, but then came the predictable cheeky answer, followed by a wave of sniggers which almost provoked a reaction from me. I smiled, thanked the comedian for his answer and asked if anyone knew an answer related to the coursework.

I had a seating plan from their usual teacher; so, I directed a question using the pupil's name. Something about the instant grin made me suspicious that they had changed seats, so that the quiet looking chap in the corner really wasn't called Liam or the girl next to him called Ryan!

When it came to writing on the board, I was anxious about turning my back to them, because these guys were a lively bunch and I knew they wouldn't behave. However, I had to use the blackboard and while I was writing, I was aware that it was all too quiet. Just then, a missile of some sort came rattling past my head. I could feel my heart pounding and I started to doubt whether I could keep control.

On to the bookwork, and the whole class claimed not to know where their text books were. As I began searching the cupboards I heard a shout and clatter. Turning round I saw one boy out of his seat, holding another pupil on the floor by his head. I let out the biggest *kiai* I have ever managed. The troublemakers were visibly startled by such a shout, as previously I hadn't even raised my voice. They returned to their seats and the whole class sat in silence for at least a couple of seconds. The textbooks were found, the fighters dealt with, and some sort of order started to return to the class. And so I survived my first lesson.

Aikido helped me a lot as I learnt to teach. *Kiai* was good for startling misbehaving children, and I found I could quite easily project my voice when I needed to. The biggest benefit of having practised aikido was the ability to stay centered amidst what can be compared to a multiple attack, when many, many things are all competing for attention. It is necessary to deal with them all in an effective manner. *Randori* had taught me that under such circumstances, it was vital to stay calm and centered, even when it wasn't all going according to plan.

Later, the ability to create space became important in my teaching, as I learned how to control the classroom environment in order to prevent problems from arising. I think this too was learnt on the mat. It helped me to deal with the student's challenges in a positive way and not stoop to the verbal attacks, put downs, or other similarly negative responses that can create a conflict between teacher and pupil. Challenges are not ignored, but are dealt with firmly and fairly. Just as with my aikido I hope that the challenger and his or her self-esteem are left unharmed by our interaction.

Ten years later, and I am now working in the primary sector and so rarely deal with anything as scary as a room full of reluctant teenage learners, but the younger pupils bring their own challenges. They are much more needy and constantly seek reassurance.

Behaviour still needs to be managed, and with the younger pupils, a skillful response to their needs is even more crucial. At times I still feel totally absorbed in the situation, dealing with challenge after challenge but careful to make space when I start to feel overwhelmed by their demands.

I do wonder if all my experience in the classroom has fed back into my aikido and made me better at *randori*. I would like to think it has.

気　気　気

Danger at Every Turn
by
Chris Woodger - Burwell Aikido Club - England - 4th Kyu

In 1999, I was diagnosed with a rare form of Gerstmann syndrome, which is a learning disability. This has certainly affected a number of aspects of my life and made things generally more difficult than might otherwise have been the case. One particular side effect is that I am very poor at assessing danger. As a consequence, the list of accidents in which I have been involved is rather long.

With this in mind, but not because of it, my partner and I started practicing aikido about two years ago, though both of us have missed classes because of injuries*(not as a result of being on the mat, I might hasten to add)* and we have both enjoyed every class. In the past, I had tried a number of other martial arts, but none had the same appeal.

One surprising consequence of my practice is that I seem to avoid a lot of the problems and accidents that would have been the norm previously. I can think of a certain occasion, when I am sure that the untrained 'me' would have been skewered by a forklift truck, but I moved as I would on the mat and got out of the way. I have also noticed that I don't bump into people nearly as often.

On another occasion, I was out helping in the work yard. I stood on a pallet that had a bit missing off the bottom. The uneven pallet rocked and I fell backwards towards the concrete ground. I feel certain that I would have been seriously hurt if it had not been for the fact that I found myself doing a backward roll, as I had learnt it on the mat. Although I was a bit shocked, I was not injured.

In short, aikido makes a big difference to my life off the mat and I am very grateful to my teachers for what they have taught me.

気 気 気

An Opening
by
Anonymous

Aikido has helped me to find my feelings and stay present when I feel threatened.

I was abused as a child and my body learned to shut down in order to survive. There was no other option for me. It took years of training in Aikido to make the connection between aikido and abuse.

I actually stumbled upon aikido. I was looking for activities for my children. I'm not much for researching topics and then choosing. Instead, I find out things from my friends and from within our community. When I was introduced to aikido, I was homeschooling my three children. I liked the idea of the kids being able to protect themselves and my sons had friends who were interested in learning aikido. A homeschooling mom mentioned a *dojo* nearby.

It was a small *dojo* and the *sensei*, a woman, was incredibly graceful in her movements. She was able to take the pent-up energy of the group of children and harness that into exercises using aikido principles. She often spoke of the philosophy of O Sensei, his strength (physical and spiritual), and she taught us some of the history. My children and I were mesmerized by these stories.

Soon I was interested in learning more, but with three kids all under eight years of age, I had little 'me time' and because my youngest was in need of constant supervision, I just stayed and watched, while my boys trained. This is how my interest grew.

After a year of observing, I knew I wanted to start training too, but like most things in my life at the time, I had to see how to make this wish a reality.

Finally, approximately two years after this thought, I began to train on the mat. I loved the rolling and flying through the air. Such freedom in my body reminded me of my love for gymnastics. Here I was in my 40s acting out my high school dream in some ways. I enjoyed the movement, the energetic awareness, and the focus on blending energies. The *aikidoka* were kind, gentle individuals who were no threat to me. I was not afraid.

As my training developed, I could see glitches in my awareness. I would skip parts of a move, rush through, or disconnect at the peak of a movement. Sometimes, I would just numb out. YUCK!!! I had hit that memory of my past. It was still raw and so unyielding. I was stuck and didn't have the awareness to label it, but it was so familiar and abrasive.

Some days I would blast through a movement; other times I would go so slow, connect with *uke*, disconnect, connect, disconnect, connect, disconnect and so on. I floated in and out of aikido, different instructors, different styles, and different sceneries. I would begin to train for months at a time. I'd make the commitment and then for some reason or another I would stop. It would take me months to re-establish that commitment again. I was constantly changing things, doing something different, but my body memory was the same. The deeper my practice became the more those uncomfortable feelings would emerge. They needed to escape.

Somehow, over time and with much self-coaxing I managed to allow these feelings to surface. It was slow! I'm not really sure how this happened, but I know aikido was my ally.

"The movement must come from your center, your core. It's all in your hips. The connection is reflected in your center," my *sensei* would say.

My "center" hadn't been talked about and observed so much, EVER! It was not used to all this attention. Perhaps that is why I needed to take these breaks in my training. I needed to go slow, have time to absorb the different sensations. Time to trust the process. Time to heal. Time to learn to blend with another person.

First I needed to find the opening, to blend with myself, my old young self, that self I had not experienced in a long time. There I was, training, opening and closing windows to my center. Memories flooding in and out, time passing and moving slowly during certain attacks or blends. All this was happening under the loving umbrella of aikido.

Time passed, I went up in grade, took another break and recently restarted my training. I am no longer intimidated by moving my pelvis, unifying with another's energy and now I can focus on movements from my core with awareness. I love the learning process that I get with the art of aikido. It has helped me to see myself and I have been able to reconnect with parts of myself that were on "life support." I am able to move energy through these areas and let it go.

The movements have a way of taking shape; they make sounds and tell stories. There are more stories of what I have done with these lessons, how I continue to grow and learn about myself and others. Aikido as an art has taught me through the movements. It has unlocked memories, painful and rewarding. It has taught me to speak up, to move, to sing and to connect. To connect not only to my *uke*, but more importantly, to connect to myself and for this I am grateful.

So what actually started as lessons in self-defense for my children became a lesson in healing for me.

Thank you O Sensei.

气　気　気

Irimi and Tenkan
by
Glen Kimoto - Aikido of Santa Cruz - U.S.A. - 5th Dan

One of the odd jobs I worked at while studying to become a teacher was that of a part-time gas station attendant. One day a large man covered in gang insignia, drove his Harley into the service area, as if to take it over. He parked in front of the pumps, strode inside, grabbed a can of wax, returned to his machine, which now blocked anyone from getting gas, and began to polish the already gleaming metal. I sensed the anger of my manager and assistant manager as they talked about it, each remark inciting a more fiery response from the other. I began to worry about the almost certain conflict between these three big men.

A Way to Reconcile the World

I had been practicing aikido for two years and had a great appreciation of the lessons of my teachers and, of course, O Sensei. 'Armed' with quiet faith and very little skill, I went out to the biker and with *'Irimi'* (entering) in mind, I met him with a friendly,

"Hi" and with sincere appreciation said, "That's a beautiful bike. What year is it? Did you rebuild it yourself?"

The biker's features melted into a soft, pleased expression as he indicated the vintage and the fact that he had indeed rebuilt it himself.

Then thinking about *'tenkan'* (turning), I asked him to pay for the wax and to polish his bike beside the building, out of the way of other customers.

There was a pause...

"That's cool," he said, and complied.

I was relieved and delighted that my aikido training had proved so effective. The manager came over afterward and looked at me accusingly.

"Hey, how come the littlest guy here can make that guy do what he's supposed to? You must know something," (as he made martial arts sounds).

"I know nothing," I replied.

Shaking his head, he turned away, mystified.

気　気　気

Knowing When to Act

by

Richard Small - Aiki Jo Bideford Club - England - 4th Dan

I was in my late forties, I guess, about the same age as my cousin; I'll call him Roger. He had invited me to join him on a rail trip around Eastern Europe and we were on the first leg of our journey. As we sat in the almost empty carriage, the cold dark evening rushed by the windows. Roger sat in front of the end wall of the carriage and I sat opposite, with a sturdy table in between us. We were sitting there quietly discussing our travels, but within half an hour trouble came our way.

For some 20 minutes we'd been disturbed by the loud voice of a violent-minded drunk, who seemed to take pleasure in pontificating about how he would punish those who he saw as wrong doers. From his vivid descriptions on what he planned to do to such people, it could easily be thought that he was a descendant of the guy who ran the dark side of the Spanish inquisition or who advised Stalin on crime and punishment.

Still, all was well, as he was engaged in educating some other poor devil behind me. Then a bad thing happened. Just by chance his eyes met Roger's, and in a split second, they transformed from casual glance into a menacing locked-in look, that operated his legs, and that carried his body to within striking distance of Roger.

"You looking for trouble?" snarled the drunk in a Barlinnie, (Glaswegian), accent.

Roger replied that, no, he wasn't looking for trouble.

"Well do you want some trouble then?" pressed the drunk.

(He would have made a good salesman, for he repeated variations of the same question over and over again). The drunk was obviously in a generous mood and prepared to hand out some free trouble to anyone who did or did not need it, including Roger, a good natured, kindly man. Roger kept looking down at the table surface, so to avoid the eyes of impending doom and retribution.

I considered the options. Stand up and whack the blighter? No, not a good idea. Stay calm and just watch as he whacks my cousin. After all, it wasn't my fight, was it? No, not too good either. In fact, it seemed best to allow the drunk to rant away until a fresh thirst came upon him and he left us for the buffet car.

From the aikido perspective, all had worked well. First, I was reasonably fit and had put in the requisite number of hours training to give me some skill and power, greater than the drunk's anyway. I had a sense of calm and it was almost as though he didn't even see me. I had maintained a good awareness throughout the incident and prepared my body and mind to affect an immobilising pin should he attack. It would have been so easy to pin his arm across the table in front of me, everything was suitably lined up. Then what? I would have had to restrain him until we arrived in London, and then let him go (unless he'd fallen asleep by then), which didn't seem likely. As the police drove me one way on a charge of assault, my train would be going in the other.

Aikido principles won the day; awareness, avoidance, distraction (by letting him focus all his venom on a defenceless cousin), whilst remaining prepared but calm. Ignoring my ego shouting at me to stand up and show him who was boss, the result was that everyone stayed safe, nothing happened and I felt good about the result.

The next train was full of football thugs going to Belgium. We adopted the aikido principle of *escape* and hid in a first class carriage, along with two railway train guards! I wonder if the guards did aikido too?

"Fear is facing your own mind and not what is coming to meet you in the alley, or waiting for you on the next train."

Beauty or the Beast

by

Quentin Cooke - Burwell Aikido Club - England - 7th Dan

My wife and I love to go on holiday in France and one particular year, before we had children, but at least a few years into my aikido training, we were staying in a rather nice holiday home in the French countryside.

It was part of a farmyard complex, complete with farmer's house, barns and a rather ferocious Alsatian dog. The beast was chained up in the yard and made a filthy noise any time we went out.

It would run towards us only to be stopped by the iron-linked chain that was attached to its collar. There it would strain every muscle to break free, barking loudly and looking, for all the world, as if it would rip your throat out, given half a chance. Even on the end of a chain, this was a little unnerving.

The dog was clearly there to protect expensive farming equipment and no right-minded burglar would think of taking it on.

It has to be said that although there were many good points about our holiday home, the dog was very low down on my wife's list of favourite things, as she doesn't like dogs, especially big dogs, and most especially big dogs that bark and snap their fangs at her. I, on the other hand, don't mind them, as I grew up with a German Shepherd and a Rottweiler. This did however, teach me to be respectful and there was no way in hell that I was going to go anywhere near this beast. Its bite definitely looked worse than its bark.

On one particular day, we were preparing to go out. My wife was a little more ready than I and had gone out ahead of me to wait by the car. I came out of the house, and noticed the dog asleep. Maybe I made a noise as I shut the front door, but suddenly it was awake and it saw my wife.

It sprang up and started to dash in her direction. To my absolute horror, I saw that for once the dog was not chained.

I was too far away to get in between, and seemingly absolutely helpless to prevent what looked like absolute disaster. It was as if time slowed down. I noted my wife rooted to the spot and frozen with fear. I saw the dog getting closer and closer as it bounded across the yard, fangs bared, snarling and barking. I could see no way to save the day, but even as I took this all in, a huge shout welled up from within and with incredible power I yelled "NOOOOOOOOOOOOOOOOOO." It was as if the dog had been struck by a missile.

It skidded to a halt, giving me time to rush forward and get between the dog and my wife. I do not recall exactly what happened thereafter, but I think I must have kept talking to the dog moving forward to ensure that it was once again chained. My shout had been a game changer and before I knew it, we had become firm friends. It seems that all the beast wanted was a little love.

So the moral of this story is that *kiai* really works. And that the dog's aggression may well have been born out of fear, as it did not take a lot of love to turn him into a good friend.

Maybe not surprisingly, my wife was not so convinced as to the dog's good character, but we had no problems after that. One final point that I sometimes ponder on is: What were the odds that my encounter should be with that most rare of hounds, a French dog schooled in English?

Aikido, Healing, and the Practice of Showing Up
by
Silvia Austerlic - Aikido of Santa Cruz - U.S.A. - 1st Dan

I started training aikido in 2004 inspired by the body-mind-spirit philosophy of Morihei Ueshiba, O Sensei. His words, *"You are here for no other purpose than to realize your inner divinity and manifest your inner enlightenment,"* spoke directly to my heart about a yearning I've been following most of my life.

Since my teenage years I've been on an eclectic spiritual journey of self-discovery and healing, fueled by the desire to claim my divine birthright and to be who I really am. I suffered from depression from early childhood and felt that my body was a place of suffering, and that the world was hostile and unsafe.

Ultimately, I decided that it was time to leave behind the 'sad story' of the first 32 years of my life. A story of not belonging, learned helplessness, and the despair of 'not having a future.' By then, I knew very well what I did not want, but not what I wanted. My dream was 'finding a community where I could share my gifts and talents,' sometime 'in the future,' in an unknown land far from home.

Seeing no way of achieving this in my homeland, Argentina, I decided to emigrate and destiny brought me to Santa Cruz in California. It took a while for me to find my feet as I embarked on a lengthy process of healing. This involved letting go of my painful past, grieving the loss of my old identity, and opening up to the possibility something new. During this process, I met a healer that supported my spiritual quest and who being a martial artist, told me that,

"Aikido is next on your path."

Naturally, I followed his advice and signed up for the beginners' class at Aikido of Santa Cruz. It was as if the doors of heaven on earth had opened for me to do this divine work.

Traumatic experiences damage us. They are experienced through our bodies and the result is that our body seems like a threatening place. This leads to disconnection between mind and body. This is how I started aikido, but aikido brought me back to my body like a shamanic soul retrieval.

Early on I was told that "the secret of aikido is to show up," and this gave me confidence, because even though this was one of the most challenging things I'd ever chosen to do, I knew I had the self-discipline to show up for one day of training at a time.

On the mat I felt safe and supported by the whole aikido community, a *dojo* culture that embodied the ideals and values O Sensei talked about. His calligraphy, *"True victory is self-victory,"* has been a constant reminder of the path ahead, offering the means, as well as the end.

Aikido has been so much more than a physical challenge. It made me question the negative self-image I'd carried for years; a false identity sustained by beliefs of disconnection, unworthiness and powerlessness. These psychosomatic patterns are ones I've needed to unlearn, to let go of again and again, in order to step into the divine self that O Sensei invites us to uncover and to express each time we step on the mat.

O Sensei said, *"Daily training in the Art of Peace allows your inner divinity to shine brighter and brighter."*

For the first time in my life, through the simple process of grounding myself and feeling my feet solid on the mat, I learned to feel safe in my body. I discovered my center and the power to 'move off the line of the attack,' away from my own negative self-limiting beliefs. I also developed the capacity to connect center-to-center with others. Simply standing in *hanmi* gave me the self-confidence to welcome the incoming energy of an attack, trusting that I'd be able to deal with it safely and harmoniously.

Furthermore, I learned that it might not be possible to stay centered all the time, but then all you need to do is develop the flexibility to fall down, the trust to self-correct, and the resilience to *"fall down seven times and stand up eight."*

Over time, I learned more about the aikido spiritual principles of *misogi*,(purification), self-correction, centering, connecting, blending, and harmonizing. I experienced them in myself and saw them embodied by *senseis* and students each in their own unique ways. I slowly understood that my job was not 'to make divinity happen,' but to become aware of all the ways in which my innate divinity had been covered by many layers of conditioning, fear and self-doubt.

In the summer of 2011, I began to focus on my *shodan* examination. My training intensified and this deepened my practice in wonderfully unexpected ways. Beyond all the self-polishing and the self-correction, an *aiki* feeling was revealed in the midst of technique. Occasionally, I was surprised by powerful moments in which my partner and I were truly in sync, in a joyous dance wherein I'd peacefully redirect the attack. My *ukes* would fall down gracefully, often laughing out loud, and evidently having a really good time. I told them that I could feel the *aiki* but did not know how to get there. They would smile in a mysterious way, telling me to keep doing what I was doing and trust.

The practice became one of not knowing, allowing myself to trust my own experience, letting go of who I think I am (my judgmental perception of what I can and cannot do), relaxing, self-correcting, harmonizing from within, and coming back to center, even in the midst of chaos, when feeling the intense challenge offered by my *uke*'s energy and not knowing what was coming next.

O Sensei said, "*Aikido is love.*" *Shodan* means first step, not a mountain-top experience, but a new beginning, a place of humility. My black belt exam came to feel like a rite of passage, an invitation to become a beginner in the mystical path of 'becoming one with the universe.' The *hakama* would just make more visible my sincere commitment to this embodied path, to keep unlearning duality, to cultivate harmonious presence, and to practice the 'Art of Peace' on and off the mat.

In my *dojo* we say that exams are 'just another day of training.' My black belt exam was a very empowering experience for me, and thankfully, on that day, it all went very well. I showed up, enjoyed the entire process, and felt grateful for every training partner who gave me the gift of their energy, so that I could polish myself and become more of my best self.

Looking back, what amazes me most is the self-confidence I now feel in all areas of my life, not because of being totally sure of what I am doing, or because I am in control of my circumstances at all times. It's just that now I know that as conflicts, challenges and crises arise, the most important thing to do is actually an inner job, to go back to center, to remember to breathe and to harmonize with what is, starting with my own self.

I can't help but smile from the heart at the amazing gift of aikido training in my life. It has taught me not to be afraid of conflict and to have a relationship with it, just as when I stay connected with a training partner, and to use this to self-correct from within. Additionally I have learned not only to follow when required, but also to lead. This is the peace-making tradition that I love and the divine lineage I am honoured to carry forth, my divinity shining brighter and brighter in my inner and outer life.

気　気　気

Caught in a Trap
by
Clair Townsend - Kinloss Ki Society - Scotland - 6th Kyu

My name is Clair Townsend, and I am a mother of five children: Sean, 14, Louise, 12, Joshua, 11, Jordan, 8, and my youngest, Skye, is 2.

My children are all of school age, but two of them are disabled. This makes life challenging. A while ago, I was finding life particularly difficult and this was putting stress on my relationship with my partner, Lee. I was feeling trapped, as we never seemed to spend time together away from the children and neither could I find any time for myself. It wasn't so bad for Lee, as he is a fitness freak, and he would go cycling or visit the gym; whereas my life is more centred around family life. The little free time I had was more likely to be spent doing a little crochet, or simply doing housework, as I like my family to be proud of our home.

In February, 2012, my family was going to expand even further, as I learnt that I was expecting our sixth child. Although I love my family with all of my heart and so was excited by the news, I knew that I had to find a way of re-connecting with the love of my life, Lee.

Sadly, things didn't turn out quite as expected and we were dealt a huge blow. In August 2012, I went to the hospital for a regular check up. Our new baby was due just after Christmas. They did some routine tests, which revealed that my baby no longer had a heartbeat. I had to give birth to my little boy, and say goodbye to him on the same day. This was very tough on both me and my relationship with Lee. I felt that it was all my fault, and my life took a nosedive.

One night, I was sitting in front of my computer browsing through a grief website, when something caught my eye. It was an advert for aikido. I clicked on the page and I was hooked. I read that aikido was more than a martial art. It was about staying relaxed and in control. It was about finding inner peace with yourself and your surroundings. I had an idea...

After discussing it with Lee, we decided to give it a go. We got a baby sitter and went along to our first class. I felt wonderful after that very first experience on the mat. I became hooked and as a result I have been able to cut down on my smoking. I have also found better ways to keep myself stress-free and relaxed. I have made so many friends and I have found something that Lee and I can do together. I really enjoy every lesson and I look forward to it every week.

Due to our family commitments, Lee and I have to do separate classes. I practice on a Sunday evening and Lee attends on a Thursday night, but after each class, whilst the children are in bed, we push the sofa back to the wall, and roll around on the carpets, doing stretches and teaching each other what we have learnt in our class. My relationship is now back on track; I am so much calmer now, and I cannot believe how aikido has managed to have such a positive impact on every aspect of my life.

It seems that at the lowest time of my life, I was sent a sign and I am thrilled that I took the chance to grab it with both hands. Still, to this day, I am loving it.

気 気 気

So Why Aikido
by
Dunken Francis - Institute of Aikido Auckland & Silverdale New Zealand - 4th Dan

At a social gathering the other day, someone asked me the question,

"Why do you practice *aikido*?"

As usual, without thinking, I fell back on my standard response,

"I started very young and I guess it has become a habit."

Since then, I have found myself going over that conversation in my mind and wondering if the answer I gave was entirely true. It was in as much as I consider it lucky that my parents moved to the end of the road where the famous 'Hut *Dojo*' was located, so that from the age of about ten I had arguably one of the best aikido masters in the U.K. (legendary H. W. Foster Sensei, one of the original students of Kenshiro Abbe Sensei), on my doorstep. But what has kept me practicing, training, and in more recent times teaching, day after day, week after week? The more I thought about this, the more reasons I came up with. So, I made a list:

1.   Aikido keeps me fit. Yes, obvious I know, but on those days when I really don't feel like training (and be honest, we all have those days sometimes). It's that internal voice that says,

"You'll be in front of a computer all day tomorrow. Get up off your butt!"

About nine years ago, I was diagnosed with diabetes. My aikido training keeps me fit, flexible, and even though it is sometimes a challenge, I believe that I am managing this 'chronic disease' far, far better than if I were not training regularly. I am what you would call a 'Type 1' diabetic, in that I have no pancreatic function whatsoever, and must inject insulin every time I eat carbohydrates. So, sometimes I'll be jabbing myself six or seven times a day. To be honest, even though this aspect of the disease is uncomfortable and can be very inconvenient, it pales into insignificance alongside the fact that pretty much every day of my life I feel pretty crappy at least once or twice a day, sometimes more.

The almost impossible task of balancing food intake with insulin doses, and then additionally to have that affected by how much activity you are doing, is such an infinitely variable and complex equation that the inevitability of feeling 'high' (a bit like feeling tired and not having had a shower for a few days, kinda itchy and irritable) or 'low' (anything from vague fuzzy-headedness to dropping unconscious and falling into a coma) just becomes part of daily life. Now add on that the occasional feeling of 'I really can't be bothered to train today,' and you start to get a picture of the mindset involved. The combination of commitment to my life as an *aikidoka* and my medical status has meant that I have to dig deep on a regular basis to fulfil my obligation to my students and to myself.

When I was first diagnosed, I reacted fairly typically. First, surprise (I've always been fit and have no diabetes in the family), quickly followed by anger and resentment.

"WHY? ME?"

Diabetes is for people who eat rubbish food, who don't exercise and who are overweight surely. Not so. It took me around a week to come to terms with my new lifestyle, and it was on the mat one evening whilst I was taking a class in *kokyunage,* when it suddenly occurred to me that this event was no different from any other shift in energy. It might be an unexpected tax bill or a wild haymaker from a drunk in the pub car park. Either way, I realised, I had to blend with it and then do my very best to turn that energy into something positive.

From then on, my entire attitude toward the illness changed and I started studying diabetes in detail. Even to the extent that my doctor referred me to a leading specialist, because she had no answers to many of my questions. By pursuing knowledge about my condition and being vigilant in looking after myself as best I could, I gradually realised where the disease's 'weaknesses' were, just like watching any opponent. I have learnt a handful of very useful strategies that enable me to live my life fully as a martial arts instructor and musician (both which often lead to long hours and late nights) and still stay healthy.

Ultimately, I have aikido to thank for this, as I suspect without its philosophy of conflict resolution hanging around in the background, I would by now be in a much worse state of both physical and mental health.

2.   Aikido keeps my self-discipline sharp. I use these words intentionally. To me, a huge part of following the *budo* way is the fact that unless you train regularly, every week, without fail, your training isn't genuine. Martial arts cannot simply be a 'hobby' that you muck about with occasionally if and when you are in the mood. It is a way, a path to follow, a chance to become more than you are, the best you can be. Every great martial artist who ever existed had a highly developed sense of self-discipline. I always imagine self-discipline as my sword. I try my best to keep it sharp by making sure I train regularly, by constantly looking for new meaning and ideas in my *aiki,* and by trying to help others become the best they can be. Without this discipline, I become dull.

3.   Aikido makes me a better person. Yes, I could write a book on this subject, but I'll keep it concise. Aikido regularly puts me in situations whether as *uke, tori* or *sensei,* wherein I have to dig deep and challenge not only myself, but my attitudes toward others, how I handle various situations and my overall perception of the world around me. I'm not saying that I don't make mistakes (Lord knows, those of you who know me will know this is true), but it does give me another ethical and emotional layer to work with, other than the simple, "Do as you would be done by," given to me by my parents. Sometimes there is no right or wrong, simply correct or appropriate action.

4.   Aikido is my family. Over the years I have met and trained with many people in many countries and I have made lifelong friends. When people join my little organisation here in Auckland, I can't help but think of them as part of the family.

Aikido training provides a very intimate and revealing environment whereby many of the facades of daily life are stripped away. This can leave people feeling very vulnerable and exposed, and it is, in my opinion, one of the roles of a *sensei* to provide a safe environment both physically and emotionally for students to train and develop in.

Over the years, I have been confided in about marriage break-ups, terminal illness, addiction, mental illness, bullying, and all manner of personal problems and traumas. I consider it a privilege and an honour that the members of my group feel they can trust me with this information, and such demonstrations of confidence only strengthen the feeling within me that we are all struggling upstream together, like salmon fighting the current.

Hand on heart, I consider many of my martial arts friends to be family. In fact, I always refer to one Eagle Claw kung fu master in the UK as 'Brother' because the bond through training and the level of sharing, support and honesty involved in a lifetime of studying martial arts together runs to the very core of our beings.

The more observant among you will have noticed that I have not mentioned 'self-defence,' and I did this on purpose. It's true that when I started back in 1974, I was a kid the same as any other, wanting to be Bruce Lee and learn how not to get bullied at school. By about second *kyu*, however, I started to realize that if I wanted a 'quick route to self-defence' I had better get a gun license. I have now wandered the *aiki* road long enough, I think, to understand some of what our art can bring to self-defence situations and also to daily life. I no longer separate the two things; they are simply aspects of a whole to be drawn upon where appropriate.

Next time someone asks me the question, "Why do you practice aikido?" I think I will answer,

"Because I am dedicated."

Actually, that's not quite correct,

"Because I am devoted. <u>I love it</u>!"

Oh Deer
by

Janet Shiel - Burwell Aikido Club - England - 5th Kyu

Sensei said to us,

"Eventually, you may find yourselves using aikido in everyday life in everything that you do."

Well, it was not long before I found out that this was true.

I was driving back from Cambridge in my little Vauxhall Tigra one foggy evening, with my partner, Chris, and two friends, Fred and Lucy. The visibility was very bad, and then suddenly through the dense, but patchy fog, appeared a very large deer. It paused on the grass verge to the right. Nothing fawn-like about this beast, it looked more like a blooming great stag.

RELAX! I thought - taking my foot off the accelerator. Lucy was screaming in the back seat, fearing we were about to crash. Fred in the front covered his face. FFF*******!!!!!!

NOW BE AWARE OF EVERTHING AROUND YOU. Hedge to the left, deer to the right, road clear ahead. It was about to cross in front of us. No time to brake!

RELAX AND AVOID THE DANGER. I waited just a millisecond.

TIMING IS EVERYTHING. Then. at the very split second it crossed in front of us, I turned the wheel to the right. We missed the animal by a hair's breadth and then I steered the car left, back to my side of the road. It was so close that we could see its white hairy belly, and the breath from its nostrils, as it seemed to fill the whole windscreen.

Waiting for the right moment to move meant that we avoided disaster. The deer was now safely on its way as were we, both parties uninjured.

With my sensei's teachings ringing in my ear, the morals of this story were clear:

Avoid conflict whenever possible.
Whatever life throws at you, try to stay calm!

気　気　気

The Best Aikido I've Ever Practiced
by
Robert Frager - Sofia University Dojo - U.S.A. - 7th Dan

Several years ago, I was training at Aikido of San Jose (California), the *dojo* of my old friend and former student Jack Wada. I was training with John, a white belt who was close to my own age. I always enjoyed working with John. He trained well and had a nice dry sense of humor. We often chatted together after class.

In the middle of our training, John suddenly changed. He put up his fists in a boxing stance and started jabbing toward my face. I didn't bother blocking his jabs, which all fell far short. I stood there my hands at my sides, dumbfounded at his behavior.

"What is going on with you?" I asked.

"Last time we trained together you hit me!" John snapped, jabbing into the air.

"I'm sorry, John. I don't think I did. If I did hit you, I apologize."

I was sure, though, that I had never struck him.

The last time I hit someone in aikido was years ago. It was shortly after I had gotten back from six months training in Shingu, Japan. My training there has been fast paced, intense, and highly martial. I brought back a lot of that focus and intensity with me. Unfortunately, when practising shortly afterwards, I overestimated the capacity of a young American training partner to respond quickly and I did strike him in the face when he left himself open. But that was a long time ago. I was positive I hadn't hit anyone since, on or off the mat.

John barked, "OK. Let's go. Let's rock and roll!"

I realized he really wanted to fight. At that moment, I could hear in my head the voices of my martially oriented Japanese aikido teachers.

"He is only a white belt and you are a fourth degree black belt. Take him out. He is disrespecting you and disrespecting aikido and he deserves it."

At the same time I realized that fighting with John would violate all the aikido ideals I had been teaching and practicing for decades. I became aware that every cell in my body was opposed to fighting with John.

I stepped back and said slowly and emphatically,

"I will not fight on the mat."

Then I turned my back on John and left him standing there, fists up, ready to fight.

I felt good about walking away. At the same time I knew if John came after me as I turned away, or if he tried to start a fight outside the *dojo*, I wouldn't hesitate to defend myself.

As I began to train with another partner, I felt adrenaline continue to course through my body. I may have seemed calm on the outside, but I was definitely unsettled inside. I hadn't been in a physical fight for decades and the whole situation seemed surreal. It felt a little bit like I was back in high school.

I could still hear my teachers' voices telling me to take John down. At the same time I knew I had done the right thing. My body knew it was right to walk away, even if my head wasn't sure.

After class I talked with Jack Wada about what had happened. He told me that John was experiencing a lot of stress in his life. He had suffered from post-traumatic stress disorder since Vietnam. Jack also mentioned that John taught some form of combat-oriented jiu jitsu and had been arrested several times for fighting in bars.

I thought to myself, "It's certainly a good thing I chose not to fight. It could have been pretty messy."

A few weeks later, I returned to the San Jose *dojo*. The first person I saw was John, who was warming up on the mat. As soon as he saw me, John came running toward me. For one tense moment I thought he was charging to attack me, but then he opened his arms and gave me a huge hug.

"Bob, you never did anything," John said "It was all me. I really need to apologize to you and also to thank you for your patience with me."
Had I become angry and fought with John, he might never have understood his anger was all about himself and not about me.

It was also a wonderful revelation to me that my body had incorporated enough of O Sensei's aikido that I knew viscerally that I had to refuse to fight. I was deeply grateful that aikido had become such a profound part of me and I realized this was probably the best aikido I had ever practiced.

気　気　気

Go Ahead, Kick Me

by

Tara Dalton - Aikido of Santa Cruz (formerly North Bay Aikido) - U.S.A.

Last summer we went to our grandma and grandpa's cabin in Lake Tahoe with our cousins, Ben and Marrisa. We had been playing together nicely until one day we were outside and Ben said to my brother Tola,

"I bet you can't kick me."

Tola said, "I don't want to kick you."

But Ben said, 'That's because you can't."

Tola didn't look at it that way.

He said,"I don't want to kick you because you're my cousin and I don't want to hurt you. Besides, this is a vacation. We're supposed to be having a good time, not fighting."

Ben said, "Go ahead, kick me. Kick me with my eyes closed."

He turned around and closed his eyes.

We decided that there was nothing else that could be said to convince him, so we went inside to make paper airplanes. A little while later, Ben came in after he had thought about it all, and made paper airplanes.

Editor's note: *Tara was aged 11 when she wrote this.*

気 気 気

Reconciling My Dark and My Light
by
Jerry Green - California - U.S.A.

The Spirit of George Leonard

The last day in January 2010 was the first day after my 67th birthday. I walked into Tamalpais *Dojo* in Corte Madera for the memorial training, honoring George Leonard who had died three weeks earlier at the age of 87. The mat was already crowded with aikido students from all over the San Francisco Bay area. The reception was filled with people greeting each other warmly.

I waded into the tiny dressing room to change into my *gi* and wrap myself in my faded brown belt. Tying the knot at my *hara* recalled the countless times over the 30-some years this ritual began my unlikely practice. In that crowded space, after taking in the eyes around me, a familiar smile once again spread heat through my body in this transition to the mat.

It took me back to my early years, recalling my childhood growing up in Sherman Oaks, constantly on guard against the approach of the bullies at my elementary school, who used to corner me and taunt me with names, while looking for an opportunity to twist my contracted left arm and shove me off balance.

As I grew up, doctors and physical therapists told me that cerebral palsy interrupted the motor functions that exerted my muscles, but didn't affect the independent function of my sensory nerves. The latter principle was only partially true, and this held me back for more than 30 years. I discovered through gestalt, massage, yoga and tai chi that sensory awareness was the key to feeling the accumulation of tension in spastic patterns, and that only through feeling the tension could I learn to release it. I could learn to settle, let go, and drop down. Hanging in with aikido for 25 years had taught me to do that in movement and under pressure, like being chased by bullies when I was young.

When the going gets tough, physically or mentally, attention rises, likely into the head where the mind can contemplate planned solutions. Aikido brought forth body wisdom under pressure, static or in movement. It trained my grounding and centering skills to operate when the heat was on, when I was being attacked. As a child, I grew up falling down. As an adult, I learned to turn falling into an art form.

It was George who had brought me into aikido and he knitted the Tamalpais aikido community together with his vision of extending its teachings beyond *dojo* walls in new and diverse forms. I recalled the day George enticed me into aikido in his tiny blue MG sports car. He'd been at Devta, the center for body awareness I'd started in Larkspur in the 70s, investigating a story he'd write for New Realities about this collection of healers, who taught yoga and tai chi. On our way to Mill Valley, he told me to feel my body weight settle into the bucket seat, receiving the pull of gravity from the core of the planet. I went deeper as he sped up along the winding road around the eastern ridge of Mount Tamalpais.

Before I lost the feeling of this thrilling and introspective ride, George took me to his basement, not far from my home and our promised destination, and shuttled me around on the mats he'd set up there to practice. He said,

"Gravity is the silent pulse of the universe, and its language is always speaking to us. The mat is like a library, where we can learn to tap into its wisdom for all our journeys."

After the memorial training, we sat in a huge circle, appreciated the moment, spread blessings of peace to our loved ones and to those suffering the world over. Then we reminisced together. I got to tell how George drove me to aikido in the sports car.

I studied with George and I trained with him. I explored his interest in applying aikido principles off the mat. He was a challenging teacher for me. After 'driving me' to the ideas of aikido, he gently 'pushed' me into a class by inviting me to stay only for the warm up and energy practices, which could last 30 to 40 minutes of a 90 minute class. I was cautious and embarrassed about my awkward physical limitations, and frightened about training with bullies. After a couple of months watching the rest of the class from the sidelines, I began to stay, and eventually train, but the challenging dynamic between us remained.

112

Little did I know how much impact this would have upon my life. On the mat I learned to deal with my physical disabilities, but in so doing it also changed my approach to life. It gave me a positive outlook and I learned that the seemingly impossible was in fact possible, if only I was prepared to put in the time and the energy. I did not see it at the time, but doors of possibility were opening, which I do not think would have been the case otherwise.

After Devta closed in 1977, *rolfer* Ed Taylor and I rented an old boat's galley for our massage and bodywork practice. Nearby in the sunlit foyer of the S.S. Vallejo, which was moored at Gate Five in Sausalito, there was a nice baby grand. In between clients, I'd sit at the piano, one-fingering its keys forlornly, and recalling this dark voice I'd often heard saying,

"You can't play music."

I had decided to study biofeedback training to explore developing my manual dexterity. I'd progressed greatly in my massage work, but I felt I'd gotten away with a lot by using my body weight more than my hands and fingers, and was ready to develop more dexterity. I'd been shopping for biofeedback equipment, thinking that it might refine my ability to feel and release my tensions. Wait a minute, if I could hear the forlorn quality in my one-fingering, was that a form of mechanical biofeedback? Did I really need sensors, buzzers and lights or expensive electronic magnification?

I tried to create a not- so-forlorn sound. This time with some breath and a relaxed, centered posture, like entering onto the mat, it sounded different. There was still this dark voice whispering,

"How can a klutz like you play music?"

But now I started hearing a second voice:

"Just be present and let *ki* play through you; expand, and let more in. *Ki* play was not at all like 'me' play. All of a sudden, there was no forlorn quality to the sound.

Something had shifted in me; something subtle, but deep. More than I could understand at the time. I began spending more time at the piano. I found out that the cost of renting my first piano was comparable to getting into biofeedback technology, so that's what I did.

I soon discovered that the easiest way to touch the keys with my left hand was with my little finger and my thumb, which sounded nicely harmonic; very nice in fact. So I just played that way with my left hand, repeating the pattern an octave up with my right hand, where I could throw in my middle finger and play a total of five notes. I was ten years into body awareness work at this point, and it didn't take long for me to try different expressions of *ki* flow, attitudes, postures and moods in which to play my own little five note arpeggio.

A music teacher who heard me said I was playing "fifths," the most common building block in harmony. No wonder the sound held some interest. She taught me to build a scale on any note, and transition through the 'circle of fifths,' which tied all keys together. All of a sudden, I started hearing intervals in popular music that were also fifths. It turns out that an 'open fifth' (without the third), was a common feature in the new age music I was listening to, such as George Winston and William Ackerman. I found a couple of favorite Winston introductions with my evolving fingering one day, and all of a sudden I was playing with his sound.

My journey in music and aikido ran in parallel. In learning to deal with my childhood demons of being bullied, which training on the mat brought back so vividly, I proved to myself that I could achieve things that had previously seemed impossible. My musical journey was also fraught with demons. When my mother brought me to a piano teacher when I was seven, I didn't last more than one lesson.

"You can't tie your own shoes, so who are we kidding,...piano?" said that dark voice.

It is probably no co-incidence that these paths merged, but now I was slowly learning to make sounds like George Winston. And that other voice was saying,

"There's way more *ki* than is in me. Get outta the way. Let it play."

Both aikido and my music helped me develop a greater self-awareness and were transforming me in remarkable ways.

By training on the mat, I learned to settle down comfortably when standing alone and then I learned to do the same when being attacked. A 'weighted touch' is also what produces a pleasant sound on piano keys and other musical instruments. Responding to attack on the mat was more challenging than collecting one's self on a piano bench, but both invited me to learn to settle down.

Before long, I was drawn to play with a few favorite themes by Ackerman, Vangelis, then some rather popular themes by Bach, Beethoven, Schumann, Eric Satie. I even co-authored a beautiful piece of music unintentionally, and I'm in the midst of another emerging composition.

Feeling my movements and listening for the sounds they create evoked a musicality in me that I couldn't have imagined. It felt just like an *aiki*-blend after opening to the 'gift' of a grab or strike. Receiving without thought and allowing things to take their own course. Yet I am a part of it. In the end, it looks and feels like my musical creation, but I still have difficulty owning that completely.

Did aikido give me the confidence to do something I thought was beyond my ability? It didn't feel like that at the time, but I would say now that it opened me to possibility. This started a surprising journey for me, which often feels like it has a momentum and direction of its own, and which has led me on a wonderful voyage of self-discovery.

You Can't Find the Light without the Dark

This book includes the famous story of *aikidoka* Terry Dobson watching an old man in *kimono* calming down an armed and drunken train robber with empathy and compassion. Yet for long after this incident, there remained in Terry a fierce anger that propelled his connections with others.

Terry was one of Morihei Ueshiba's closest students and assisted O Sensei personally in tasks of daily living. I took a liking to him immediately, and we became friendly on and off the mat, often chatting over shared experiences at California's pioneer growth center, Esalen Institute, and our shared interest in aikido, kabbalah, and playing chess. Somehow I got close to him in spite of my discomfort with his tough-guy brashness.

I attended his pioneering psycho-drama workshops on using *aiki* in conflict situations. He was crude and awkward with words, but fascinating and inspiring in his search for mind-body connection. I loved him up, and he liked me, or the attention I gave him, perhaps both.

At least that was the case until the night that he shared teaching a class with Richard Strozzi-Heckler. In the middle of class, Terry broke in to my partner practice and extended his wrist to me. After a couple of tries to take his wrist, he taunted me by saying,

"Why are you such a fucking slow learner, Green?" and then he stormed off.

He came back after the next demonstration to take me on again. There I was, still a fresh brown belt mesomorph, off guard again, feeling quite vulnerable to an angry 250 pound black belt commanding the respect of my *sensei*. This time I said meekly that I had some ideas as to why I might be "such a slow learner." He listened up.

I said, "I'm still insecure in my body because of my congenital limitations and that inhibits my learning this quickly. And, quite a separate thing is that your anger frightened me, and I was frozen in my own fear."

He seemed to grow even angrier and came right at me declaring loudly,

"You see anger, then you purify it!!!" and he whacked me where it hurts with the back of his hand. I wasn't injured, except for my pride, just in pain.

We'd created enough commotion to get Richard's attention, but not enough to interrupt the class. I got off the mat, feeling disillusioned and humiliated. Richard came over and asked if I was okay.

I said, "Probably but I need to sit-out some."

I couldn't say more.

Later, I asked Richard to convene a *dojo* meeting to discuss anger and other negative training attitudes on the mat. Terry was invited but he did not attend. Nor was he at the *dojo* for a while thereafter. Long enough to notice, but not more than a couple of weeks. Then one night after a rigorous practice I came down the big iron staircase into the darkened parking lot, carrying my sweat-soaked *gi*. There he was, shoulders hunched and again he seemed angry.

"Green, you're trying to run me outta town...!?" Terry growled.

"No," I said, as he grabbed me with both fists, pulling me close. "I'm looking for a way to train with you and feel safe about it, Terry."

He tensed again, and my favorite Eddie Bauer chamois snap-fastened western shirt ripped straight up the left side of my chest. We were nose to nose. I was close to soiling my pants. That was the only sense of 'settling down under pressure' that I could feel.

Terry paused and seemed to reflect on what his anger had wrought, then opened his fists, releasing the tattered edges of cloth to drop upon my pounding chest.

Shortly after that, Terry left town for the East coast. I didn't know when, as I hadn't come to the *dojo* for a while, and I felt a bit out of the loop. Then one evening I came in to train. As I approached the counter, Richard set out before me a wrinkled brown paper bag, crumpled closed, and bearing in black marking-pen a message saying, "To Jerry, with love from Terry." Richard wondered if I might open it now since,

"We are all curious to see what's inside..."

I opened it. Inside was a round steel gear-piece with a rusty sprocketted perimeter, sharp in some places, and just where I picked it up. A drop of red curiously appeared on my finger; no pain, but I was bleeding. Inside the hard steel circle (also an aikido symbol of harmony/love) was the tattered paperback '9½ Mystics' by Herbert Weiner', my first read in the study of Kabbalah that I'd loaned to Terry many months ago, when he'd expressed having a common interest in Jewish Mysticism.

I kissed my finger until the bleeding stopped. It was time for class. Terry wasn't around. Or was he? That night I began to feel deeper into my own darkness for my own light.

Kabbalah teaches that light was created from within darkness. Mysticism is indeed mysterious and to me aikido has often felt the same. What Terry taught me through his basic humanity and obvious struggle with his own demons was that in order to change you had to look deep within. He wasn't the only teacher to make this clear to me, but he reached parts of me that no one else could have.

After that class, I carried that wrinkled shopping bag full of Kabbalah and bloodied steel down the *dojo* stairs into the darkened parking lot where I'd last seen Terry Dobson. It was just a book and a steel ring, but the contents meant more than I could comprehend that night. He hadn't been on the mat, and neither was he in the parking lot, but I felt his presence strangely within me.

A long time passed before Terry returned to teach again in Point Reyes for one of his last moments on the mat. A mutual friend encouraged me to come by, saying frequently that Terry wanted to see me again. We met after the training in the hallway by the kitchen and greeted one another in silence, holding both hands gently, gazing into one another's eyes, and no words needed to be said.

Terry taught me something really important, that we all have faults, even renowned teachers, and that we can't ignore that side of ourselves. We have to face our demons and deal with them as Terry so publicly did. His honesty touched me deeply and enabled me to see that my own limitations were the very thing that I could learn the most from.

Taking Evasive Action
by
Patrick Carsons - Aikido of Columbus - U.S.A. - 1st Dan

Aikido recently kept me from serious injury. I have been practicing aikido for 15 years and never imagined that it would help me to avoid a car accident. I had just visited my local Walmart to pick up some new eye glasses. I was driving around the outer lanes of the shopping center and came to a stop sign.

The incoming traffic had two lanes and you could either turn left or right. There were some bushes by the stop sign, which made it difficult to see if there were any cars on my right side. I started to pull out, and all of a sudden I saw a car approaching. The driver slammed on his brakes. The car right in front of me stopped where I would be sure to hit him. Not a good move!! Without thinking, I turned the steering wheel as fast as I could and skidded to the rear of the stopped car. Actually, it was like the classic two-step turn we practice in aikido. I angled my car to match the angle of the car stopped in front of me, and that allowed me to miss hitting him, - just barely.

I had managed to get all the way around the rear of the first car when I felt something coming at me. I pushed the gas pedal all the way to the floor and accelerated out of the intersection. Sure enough, there was a second car that I had not seen in the other lane. Somehow, I had felt its presence and had known just how to blend with this vehicle too. There were no collisions, only the honking of horns.

What I find most interesting about this event is that I remained very calm throughout. It was like being on auto-pilot; my body just took over and did what was needed to stay safe.

In aikido, we often practice defense against multiple attackers, and this has taught me not to let my mind get stuck on any one attacker, but instead to be aware of the whole space rather than any one person. The foundation for that wide-open perception is learning to stay calm under pressure. In aikido, we do exercises working with breathing, posture, and intention to create that calmness. The good news is that this works off the mat, as well

119

as on it. The results of such practice certainly saved me and the people in the other cars from any harm.

Blocked
by
Jim Hammond - Jikishinkan - England

As I drove out from where I lived to take my wife to a doctor's appointment, the road was blocked by some cars. I parked my car and went over to see what was wrong. On reaching the front of the queue, I found two cars that couldn't move until one of them reversed a couple of feet. If he did so, we could all then be on our way. One of the two drivers didn't have an option to move, but when he asked the other car driver to move, he was told to "Fuck off!" Despite all logic, the other driver would not move.

I went to the window of the other driver's car and said,

"Do me favour, mate. Would you move back a couple of feet, as my wife has a doctor's appointment?"

"Fuck off! " he replied. "I'm not moving."

I then walked round and opened his passenger door and asked again. His reply was the same and he added,

"Get your hands off my property. You have no right to touch my car."

I was quite angry and slammed his door shut, but decided to walk away and leave it at that. As I did so, he came rushing out of his car asking me what was I going to do about it. I adopted my basic aikido stance, with my hands up, with my right foot forward and knee bent and waited to see if he would attack, whilst ensuring that I kept a safe distance between us. To my surprise, this seemed to give him pause for thought and he then put his hands in his pockets and just stood there. So I walked away feeling calm and not under any threat. I went back to my car and within a few minutes all the cars moved and I was on my way.

Three or four days later, I was driving out of my turning and there was a lorry picking up a large container full of rubbish. Once again, the road was blocked, and coincidentally, the same ill-mannered driver who had behaved so badly just a few days before was in front of me. As I stopped, he obviously saw me, because he got out and walked back to my car. I wound down my window and to my surprise he offered me his hand, which I shook.

He apologised for his earlier behaviour and explained that he had buried his wife the day after the incident. He told me that at the time he had wanted me to hit him. I held his hand for over a minute, whilst I assured him that I would not have done so unless he made a move to attack me. A real connection formed between us at the end of which he got in his car and drove off.

After hearing his story, I was so pleased that I had stayed calm, when he came at me and I am sure that this was only because of my 12 months aikido training, given by my teacher, Sensei Simon Hirst. Aikido had made me a calmer person and for this I am extremely thankful.

気 気 気

Aikido and Embodiment
by
Wendy Palmer - Aikido of Tamalpais - U.S.A. - 6th Dan

People often ask me why I decided to start aikido. I can only say it wasn't a rational decision. Why does anyone engage in a love relationship? Aikido is an art of beauty, power and grace. The fluid and complex movements are at once natural and exotic - I was attracted; it was love at first sight. Falling in love is mysterious and irrational and my experience is that there is always something to learn if we open ourselves, face our fear and work humbly with our desires. My desire was to be able to control my energy and yes, at first the energy of something bigger than me, the energy of my partners. My fear was that I would be controlled and that I would be out of control.

Practicing on the mat allowed me to experience my fears and desires directly in my body without words. I couldn't talk my way out of it. So little by little I learned to open to the intensity and began to find ways to control myself. I started to understand that controlling myself was more important and more powerful than controlling others. Practice is not a question of accomplishing self-control or gaining mastery, working with one's own energy is not a goal, it is a journey over a lifetime.

I have been practicing aikido for over 40 years. Over these many years aikido has been a teacher, partner, lover, adversary, path and a lens to observe how we humans engage with each other in the laboratory of simulated stress. I have seen that we are loving, tender, defensive, aggressive, fearful and unbelievably generous. The conditions created by the container of the mat; bowing, grabbing, striking, throwing and falling are a theater of life, expressing itself in the ideas of non-violence, compassionate power and reconciliation in a simulator of controlled aggression. I have learned much and have much to learn and I continue to be grateful for this extraordinary art that has enriched my life beyond my wildest dreams.

I am now using the principles I have gleaned from my years on the mat to inform and shape the work I do as a coach and in the Leadership Embodiment (LE), work, training others to use those principles and practices to coach and facilitate people in organizations and their lives.

How Leadership Embodiment Evolved

For as long as I remember, I've been fascinated by how some people are able to easily influence people and situations, while others struggle to get a response from their efforts.

When I was young, I loved horses and had some wonderful experiences riding and training my own and my friends' horses. Through these experiences, I saw that non-verbal behavior affects interactions more than words. In school, I learned about great leaders who changed the world and I wondered how they were able to do it. Those leaders seemed to have an expansiveness that included entire nations as if the whole nation was their family. I wondered how they were doing that because I had to work so hard to sustain my connection with just three other family members.

I started paying attention to the posture and gestures of effective people and began to see patterns that were repeated in a variety of situations. I studied the non-verbal communication of countless people that included animal trainers, politicians, business leaders, military commanders and spiritual leaders. I observed that those who were truly effective shared common ways of standing, sitting, gesturing in relationship to themselves and others, especially in challenging and complex situations. These observations were enhanced through my study of the non-aggressive martial art of aikido and practicing mindfulness meditation.

As I simultaneously studied aikido and mindfulness, I looked for the underlying principles governing the capacity to be effective in stressful situations.

Aikido has always given me great metaphors for leadership. Aikido has shown me what a centered, powerful leader can accomplish in situations of conflict and overwhelming odds.

In aikido we say that, "It is not the size of your biceps but the size of your spirit that makes the difference in how the conflict is resolved." When a leader is centered, their spirit expands their personal space to include their environment and everyone within it.

The study and practice of aikido offers real 'in-the-moment' opportunities to practice and deal with stress and confusion. Aikido allowed me to learn how to fall skilfully, not just physically, but emotionally and psychologically as well. Falling and standing up in a new position without stress or judgment is one of the gifts my body received from aikido training. We call it "the art of falling."

My whole being learned how to recover, adapt, and go forward within situations that are continually unfolding.

Many great leaders have said that they learn more from their failures than their successes and that their failures lead to success. This quote from

Michael Jordan testifies to his relationship to failure, "I've missed more than 9000 shots in my career. I've lost almost 300 games. Twenty six times, I've been trusted to take the game winning shot and missed. I've failed over and over and over again in my life. And that is why I succeed." One of my favorite poets, Rainer Maria Rilke says, "The purpose of life is to be *defeated by greater and greater things.*"

I believe that balanced leadership gives us the ability to step out of the deep-seated desire for security, and the need to fix things and into our full potential. The centered leader is brave and can welcome both success and failure with complete openness.

Powerful, centered leaders have a capacity for working with intensity without constricting. On the aikido mat this translates as the ability to skilfully manage impact. The impact is physical and we learn how to deal with it without collapsing or becoming aggressive. In aikido we speak of receiving the attack. We learn to relax and allow the resilience of our body and our personal space to become shock absorbers.

Translating the concept and practice of receiving the attack into the psychological and emotional arena of leadership has been challenging, but has yielded some of the most useful LE techniques.

On the mat we learn by feeling the relaxed power of our teachers. Then, little by little over years, we develop our ability to relax and open while receiving impact. On the mat we invite attacks so that we can practice, grow stronger, and develop capacity for tolerating the hit or grab with relaxation and openness.

In everyday life the impact we experience comes in the form of words and thoughts. In LE training, we use partner and group interactions as we do on the aikido mat to simulate stress. Rather than strikes and grabs, we use words, gestures and mild physical pressure to simulate impact, so that we can practice dealing with intensity and learn more skillful responses. During these exercises of simulated impact and stress, we examine posture, muscle group usage, and the quality of attention. We work with LE tools to practice relaxing and opening in the face of stress; we grow stronger as we develop our capacity for managing the negative connotations of words and thoughts.

The Possibilities are Endless

For those of us lucky enough to be able to practice aikido on the mat, we must not lose the awareness of how truly fortunate we are. It is a great blessing that we have been given a body that can practice, a mind that is open to the teachings and a spirit that is willing to investigate beyond the deep desire for self-protection. Not everyone is so fortunate, yet everyone can benefit from the concepts and principles that are the essence of the art.

When I bring the aikido principles to people through the context and forms of LE, I am often delighted to find them latent or already manifesting in the work people are doing for their self-development. Aikido principles are universal and can be used to empower people of all ages, colors and abilities.

There is wonderful work being done in the world, some of it is more formal, with clear language and exercises that connect to the physical training we learn on the mat. Organizations like Aiki Extensions offer a rich variety of methods for a wide range of situations.

It is inspiring to find places where the principles exist in traditions that are completely different from the direct lineage of O Sensei. In South Africa the Truth and Reconciliation Committee has been a beautiful example of offering a way to 'protect the attacker' from creating further suffering for themselves and others. In Bhutan the notion that we live our lives in order to dedicate 'all our actions for the benefit of all beings' is an inspiring example of the notion of '*budo* as love.'

The possibilities are endless and I know that if we open our hearts and minds with the intention of discovering the spirit of aikido in unexpected places. we will find the beauty, power and grace of this marvellous art woven into the fabric of human life. Recognition and acknowledgment of this spirit helps it grow and energy organizes around what is most articulate in a system. In this spirit let us keep the stories coming, keep the practices going and growing and be grateful for the opportunity to share our experiences with the world.

気 気 気

Healing with *Ki*

by

Richard Moon - Aikido of Marin - U.S.A. - 6th Dan

It was almost light out. I heard voices. Awakening in a strange room, slowly I remembered that I was visiting my mother. It took me a minute to assemble myself. She and my father had divorced many years before and she now lived in San Diego. "That's right", I thought. I was at my mother's apartment in San Diego. I had brought my eldest son down to visit her.

She always woke up early, but it didn't make sense that she'd have visitors at quarter to six in the morning. I dressed quickly and went towards her room. Her door was ajar and she was talking with my Auntie Anne. They were discussing something important. I backed away to leave them alone when my mother noticed me.

"Richard," she said, her voice sounding strained, "come in."

There was an eerie silence that I couldn't place on entering the room.

"I've got bad news," she quivered. She lowered her voice; there was a pause. "Gene called. Bill was in an accident."

Gene is my younger brother and a doctor. Bill is my older brother and a wild card.

"Gene didn't want me to be alone and I didn't want to wake you. So I called Auntie Anne."

Anne had a hard look on her face. That worried me. There weren't too many things she took that seriously. My mother confirmed my suspicions.

"It's serious," she said. "Gene's afraid he's going to die."

Bill had been stopped at a stoplight on his scooter. A drunk hit him from behind. The guy said he never saw Bill, who wasn't wearing a helmet. Much later, I found out he had flown about 30 feet through the air, and his scooter had been completely demolished. He was unconscious. They had to drill holes through the cranium to relieve the pressure caused by the bleeding that threatened his brain. I looked at my mother through the heavy silence that filled the room. There was an internal stillness from the rush of emotional energy and numbness that accompanies shock.

One aspect of the study of aikido is the development of trusting the inner sense or intuition. Out of this vast ocean of inner quiet, words formed and I found myself saying, "He'll be alright." I said it assuredly almost as if someone else were speaking. They looked at me as if to say I seemed naive.

Bill had been taken to Hennepin County General. This was where my younger brother had done his residency. Since he knew many of the staff there, Gene had spoken to the doctor in charge.

The head trauma was severe. The next 24 hours would be critical. No one knew if Bill would live. He was in the intensive care unit on life support systems. If he held on for 24 hours, there was a good chance his vital signs would stabilize, but there was still no telling when, or if, he would wake up. And if he did, who would he be?

Maybe the reports were exaggerated. At any rate, they didn't match my inner feelings, which still said Bill would be all right. Of course there was also a part of me thinking that maybe this was just denial, an inability to face the truth. I was planning to fly home to the San Francisco Bay Area that morning. My son was staying and Auntie Anne would be there. There was little more to do for my mother.

I went home and waited, every moment expecting good news. Days passed. Nothing. It became a week. Still nothing. Once Bill survived the first critical period, it was much less likely he would die in a coma. But whether he'd wake up and the nature of damage to the brain was still unknown.

All my mother's friends expected her to take the first plane to Minneapolis, but Gene really discouraged her. At least at home she'd be comfortable and have her work. If she went to Minneapolis there'd be nothing for her to do but sit by the hospital bed and worry. After a week and a half she called and said she was going. She couldn't wait any longer. She flew in on Friday to be there for Bill's birthday. He turned 40 in a coma.

A couple of days later she called and said that on Sunday, when they were all at the hospital, Bill seemed to have fluttered his eyes. Gene said, "If you can hear me, blink." They all imagined he had responded, so they asked him again. When they felt he repeated the response the first ray of hope streamed into our lives.

Excited, I left on a trip looking forward to better news when I got back. Maybe Bill would be fully awake.

But the message on my return was that there'd been no further response. Maybe there had never been one. If anything, Bill was sinking deeper. Something sank inside of me too. Fear started to overcome me for the first time about how serious the situation really was. I'd been so sure that Bill was going to be all right. The sureness was waning now. A fog of depression settled around me.

Visibly upset I stopped by to see a friend and told him my story. He couldn't believe I hadn't gone back to Minneapolis. Being so sure that Bill would be all right, I hadn't even considered it. Even though there was nothing I could do for Bill, he thought I should go back just to take some of the pressure off my family, to make it easier on them in some way. Maybe someone else would have handled it that way, but it didn't feel right for me. It did, however, start me thinking again about going back to Minneapolis. This thought stayed with me through the night and it woke me up the next morning. My sense of concern was growing.

At one point, in the depths of depression, I imagined trying to make contact with my brother, and again some very rational part of me wondered if it was only an indication of the toll the stress was taking on me.

In my imaginary construct of the universe I liked to think it was Bill's choice about whether or not he came back. "Bill," I thought, "It's up to you. It really is your life. Sure you feel us all pulling on you, but it is your decision. Come back if you want to come back. But don't come back to make it easy on me or mom or anyone else. It will be hard enough if you come back wanting to be here. If you do it any other way, I'm afraid it will be torture for all of us. It's your choice, Bill. Be full in it."

Suddenly, I imagined him not coming back. The time prior to the accident had been very hard for him, and this might have affected his spirit. I learned much later from my brother Gene that the present medical theory regarding coma was that people woke up when they were ready. There was nothing that could be done about it. His opinion, however, differed slightly from this view. He felt that attention, familiar voices, stimulation, and pain were of value in bringing the awareness to a state of consciousness.

All at once the image of having to tell people, "I had two brothers, but one went into a coma and never came out," began to work its effect on me. Imagining saying this as if it had really happened I suddenly felt the responsibility to go and be with him, to tell him that I wanted him back, and to lend my energy for his recovery. I didn't know where this impulse came from. It didn't really feel like me. My friends in 12-step programs like AA might call it my Higher Power. Anyway, the feeling persisted. I felt something was being asked of me.

I teach aikido and in my class that night, as often happens, the details of my personal life fade. Still, since I don't get into fights and there is no competition in aikido, the real power of the training is its application in daily life. As I drove home after class, thoughts of my brother grew stronger and stronger. The impulse calling me to be with him intensified. Enumerating all the reasons not to go, I found myself calling the airline about 10 that night. There was a midnight flight that arrived in Minneapolis at 6:00 a.m.

My mother planned to leave Minneapolis and fly home in the morning, so I called her, thinking she might change her plans if she knew I was coming. She told me she was exhausted. She would return to Minneapolis when Bill woke up but she was going home in the morning.

Apparently, she called Gene, because she called me later after talking to him. They both felt it made no sense for me to come now. She said they thought I probably could do more for Bill when he woke up. Perhaps she was talking more to herself while she tried to dissuade me from coming.

I felt myself in an emotional spin. I had felt so strongly moved to go. But my mother and Gene so emphatically tried to dissuade me. I looked inside but was losing the clarity to act. I felt lost.

The thought of flying in like some idiot on a big white horse, and charging into the hospital for no reason, made me feel foolish about wanting to go. Still the impulse driving me to go seemed to overcome my fear. What I would like to emphasize here is that the feeling that was the hardest to deal with was the sense that there was something within my power that could be done, and that it was imperative that I go. I asked Carol, the woman in my life, for guidance. She returned me to my own source.

"It doesn't matter what they think. You're the one you have to live with. Follow the course that you'll like yourself best for."

I called the airlines, booked a flight. Then I called my mother to tell her I was coming. She seemed frustrated, but I told her she could go home or stay according to her needs but I would be there at 7:00 a.m. She hung up, but called back 10 minutes later to say she would stay and be there to pick me up at the airport.

I got on the airplane and fell asleep. I dreamed about Minneapolis and my past. The dreams were vague but echoed feelings of the pressures of youth, the communication or lack thereof with my father and of a wild childhood and running away at 16 to 'find myself.' Ever since I had chosen an unorthodox path for my life, there had been an unspoken strain between my father and me. My younger brother had taken up an intelligent profession as a doctor. I had been out on the coast, goofing off, studying this weird martial art, which my father regarded as worthless.

I woke up as we touched down. It had been a long time, but the airport looked the same and the air felt familiar. As I walked through the airport, my awareness was flooded with memories. Somewhere between the tiredness and the power that had brought me to Minneapolis was a sense of a greater knowledge guiding me. As I stood outside the airport in a daze, my mother drove up.

Even though it was still early morning, the sultry heat of summer's end was already flooding the city. We talked about Bill, Minneapolis, the family, and the issues surrounding the accident. All the time we talked, anxiety and pressure were building within me.

We finally pulled up in front of the hospital. As we moved through the lobby, the reality of what we were facing pressed in on me. Bill had been lying there unconscious for almost a month, surrounded by people bustling about in their activity and he was oblivious to all of it. The energy within me pulsated and the pressure of some unknown force increased. My heart was pounding. It began beating faster and louder. It is hard to explain the tension I felt between feeling lost and being there. To use the words of the founder of aikido, I felt as if on a "bestowed mission."

We took the elevator upstairs and walked past rooms filled with machines, past nurses and orderlies with their carts. Someone was wheeled past us on the way to surgery. It was trance-like, almost a dream. With each step it got more real and unreal at the same time. The intensity, the energy and the anxiety continued to grow stronger.

Somehow, I expected the process to be more gradual when my mother turned me toward one of the doorways. We stepped into the room and there lay the unconscious body of my brother, Bill. I mean he was alive but he wasn't there. I noticed small movements on the right side; his left side was paralyzed. His head moved very slightly, as if he were dreaming. There were low, unintelligible growling sounds coming from him. I stood there with no conscious idea of why I was there or what I had come to do.

This may sound a bit Californian, but indulge me. I soaked up the energy in the room as it merged with the energy in my own system. This is a combination of sensing, feeling, an almost meditative or mystical (meaning I can't explain it) receiving of sensory impressions and intuitive guidance. The mystery of what I will call the guidance of spirit was the reason I had been drawn to the study of consciousness arts like aikido, Zen and yoga.

I watched the nurses move him like a big doll. They put a tube through his nose down into his stomach. No response. There was a needle in his arm and an oxygen mask on his face. They cleaned him; they dressed him; and all the time they moved around him, they talked to him with no response.

The pulsation of energy within me intensified, pounding louder, stronger, faster.

There was a resident in the room making his rounds. After being introduced to me he yelled into Bill's ear,

"Bill, your brother Richard is here."

What did he have to lose? Nothing.

All but one nurse left the room. My mother was still there and my brother's friend Christine came into the room. As they both stood by the foot of the bed, I gradually moved closer. I put my hands on him, one hand by his neck and one hand on his face. I talked to him and called to him but got no response.

The word *ki* in *ai ki do* means life energy or vital force. In my study of aikido, because of my nature or interests, I've given extensive attention to the process of *ki* healing. I've done so by taking extra seminars and seeking out information and teachers focused on it.

Ki healing is the practice of consciously flowing *ki*, or life energy, to an injury in order to stimulate the healing process. A mother kissing a child who is hurt is an example of the transference of *ki*. I had used *ki* healing a number of times, but never in a situation like this. Though skeptical of my own impressions at first, I experienced the flow of *ki* akin to a golden, honey-like substance. Even with all my years of training, I was impressed with how tangible the experience felt.

From the same mysterious realm of awareness that had brought me there in the first place, I was moved to take Bill's hand and apply the form of an aikido technique called *nikyo*, a wrist joint lock. *Nikyo* has the potential of creating pressure to the point of intense pain. All aikido techniques can be traced back to martial conflict, but the way I applied the technique now, was different.

I was sending the energy flowing through the technique as a way of contact with the center of his being. In this approach to the art, my attention was attuned to the sense of *ki* or energy flow, I continued. After

132

a moment it seemed as if his eyelids began to flutter and his eyes seemed to move as if looking for something.

I asked, "Bill, Bill, can you hear me?"

Though the sound came from deep in his throat and was very garbled, not at all clear, I could have sworn he said, "Yeah." Admittedly I wanted to hear him say something so badly that I couldn't be sure. Afraid I was making it up, I put the *nikyo* on stronger; and flowed more energy through him. His eyes were definitely responding. I was sure of it now. I said,

"Bill, who am I?"

Almost unintelligible in garbled tones, from very deep in his throat, he said, " . . ichard."

I looked around the room. The nurse's eyes were wide open. My mother and Christine still stood at the end of the bed. They were holding each other and had a look of wonder in their eyes. They both nodded.

Christine said, "I'm sure he said, 'Richard.' I'm sure he said your name."

You would have to have been there and heard how unintelligible his speech was to understand the twilight zone we were in at that moment.

I turned back to Bill and applied the *nikyo* again. I asked, "Bill, can you feel this?"

He said, "Yeah."

Each time he spoke, the words seemed to get just a little clearer. I said,

"Bill, say my name."

When he said "Richard" this time, we all looked at each other. We were afraid to believe it, yet we all seemed sure we had heard him speak. I brought the pressure up more. I said, "Bill, if this hurts, say uncle." In a voice that was garbled yet distinctly a word, he said "Uncle." It was loud and clear. That time none of us in the room questioned it. We looked at each other through tears, laughter and smiles.

The nurse stopped what she was doing in shock. She looked at me with very large eyes and said, "What are you doing?"

I explained my interest in the art of aikido as the study of life energy. I told her that it was used for healing as well as self-defense. I told her that I was in the process of transferring *ki* or healing life energy, into my brother and that I was using this process to make contact with his awareness.

She looked at me politely. I could almost hear her thinking that one of the two of us must be crazy, and since I was from California, there was little question of who she thought it might be. At the same time, she'd been there and seen him respond. She left the room suddenly.

My mother was in tears. She ran to the phone to call Gene who was finishing up a residency at the Mayo Clinic in Rochester. When she came back, she said he'd gotten someone to cover his rotation there and that he was leaving immediately. He and his wife would be in the Twin Cities in a couple of hours.

It was probably less than five minutes before a battery of doctors walked into the room. The nurse had probably said something that brought them so quickly. They'd been with Bill for more than four weeks and had seen no conscious response. They walked around Bill. They poked him; they prodded him. They talked to him, no response.

Bill had meanwhile drifted back into his unconscious state and made no clear response. They saw nothing. I felt they were watching me out of the corners of their eyes but said nothing, so I said nothing. Looking at me again, they left the room.

Just as they were leaving, my father unexpectedly walked into the room. He hadn't known I was coming and was quite surprised to find me there. He'd been to the hospital every day since the accident. The strain showed on his face. He said that yesterday he had hit rock-bottom. After all this time of nothing he had lost hope. He said he spent the night on the verge of tears, afraid Bill would never come back. My mother interrupted him.

"Jay," she said, "Bill just said Richard's name."

I walked over to the bed and took my brother's hand again and applied the *nikyo*. His eyes started to roll. His eyelids started to flutter and then open. He seemed to be looking around the room.

"Bill, do you know who is in the room now?"

He didn't respond immediately, so, I asked him again, "Bill, who's in the room now?"

In his deep, garbled almost unintelligible voice, he said, "Dad."

It wasn't clear, but it was clear enough. Joy streamed from my father.

"I can't believe it," he said. "It's incredible, just incredible."

He kept repeating his response. As we say in California, his mind was blown. For a moment at least, the study of aikido seemed to have tangible value.

No one really knew what had happened. It didn't really matter. The fact that Bill had responded was enough for us at the moment.

I asked him one more time to say my name and he did. The thrill and excitement in the room were so intense I can still feel it. Bill drifted back to sleep. As my father sat by the bed, my mother and I went out to breakfast.

By the time we got back, Gene was there. He had gotten no response from Bill to his attempts to reach him. He asked me what had happened. I went to Bill's side and took his hand and started the process to awaken his consciousness using the power of aikido. When Bill began to show signs of surfacing, I said,

"Bill, Bill, tell me who's in the room now?"

He said in that deep very garbled tone,

"Brother Gene."

It was a beautiful experience to be with Gene at that moment.

Now my younger brother is a bit of an enigma. He has had experience with meditation and other realms of consciousness. Initially, some of his interest in medicine had included some of the more ancient healing techniques, including acupuncture, herbal medicine, and pressure point therapy. He intended in his study to research how they fit into the body of modern Western medicine. In the years he had been training as a doctor the training caused his views to become more conservative. I did not know how he would see what had happened.

Medical science and modern technology would have to look on it as coincidence that Bill woke up in my presence. It is a dilemma. We don't want our doctors to be closed-minded, but we don't want them living in 'fantasy land' either.

I guess his curiosity got the best of him. At any rate, he asked me to show him what I was doing and explain the process to him, as I understood it. After I did, he stood on one side of Bill and I stood on the other. We each took one of his hands. We began the process, gradually increasing the *ki* flow and stimulation. I encouraged Gene to feel the energy flowing through him into Bill, even if he thought he was only imagining it. As we continued the process, gradually Bill began to wake up more and more.

"Bill, can you see us?"

His voice was deep and garbled, but he said, "Yeah."

I said, "Bill, do you know that we're here?"

He said, "Know you're here." Or did he say, "Know we're here?" Was he responding or was he simply repeating the words that he had heard? Was he thinking or was he just parroting? Rephrasing the question. I asked,

"Bill, do you know who I am?"

He said, "Know who you are."

Gene and I looked at each other and at that moment we knew that Bill was with us, that he was hearing us, that he understood us, and that he could make an intelligent response. He was not just mimicking the words, but he could conjugate the verb from 'who I am' to 'who you are.' My father was concerned that we were hurting Bill. He wanted us to stop. We let Bill go back to sleep. My mother, my father, Gene and I went out to lunch.

It was a pretty exciting gathering for all of us after the tension of the last month. For Gene especially, who because of his medical training had the greatest knowledge and therefore the greatest fear that Bill would be a vegetable, the excitement was overwhelming. Gene kept saying,

"He is going to be alright. Rutabagas don't talk."

What a difference it was, not to be wondering if Bill would wake up or be able to think. Now we were thinking in terms of how much would he recover. How much would his mind come back? Would he recover the use of his arm and leg? How long it would take? We started dreaming of total recovery. We had all come a million miles from where we had been a few hours earlier.

After lunch Gene and I drove my mother to where she was staying so she could take a nap. Then we headed back to the hospital. Word must have spread like wildfire, because when we walked back into Bill's room there were six of his friends there. They had been trying to talk to him with no response. It was obvious they were wondering whether or not anything had really happened.

Gene and I looked at each other. We moved to opposite sides of the bed. He took one hand and I took the other. We started the *aiki* process of stimulation. We began flowing energy into Bill through the technique. Everyone in the room squirmed. They were afraid we were hurting him. Some of them even made comments to that effect. Ignoring them, I concentrated my attention on the sense of energy flow into Bill's body, into his mind, and into his being. His eyes began to move and gradually to open. They seemed to roll about the room and his sounds were louder.

I said, "Bill, can you see who's in the room?"

He said, "Yeah." A ripple of excitement went through the room. At the time two of Bill's closest friends, Larry Marcus and Stevie Kaplan were in the room. Stevie's mother had died the week before Bill had been hit. Feeling overwhelmed, he had been unable to visit while Bill was in a coma because the emotional strain had been too heavy for him. The weight of the sadness he felt was evident.

I asked again, "Bill, who is in the room with us?"

His eyes rolled around the room once more. There were some gurgling noises again and then he said fairly clearly, "Kaplan."

The excitement in the room was so thick you could cut it with a knife. Stevie started to cry. No one could believe it. We all shared in the joy.

The feeling was overwhelming, because it seemed there was power in the aikido, and through that power we had been able to establish communication with Bill. Shortly, he began saying my name and Gene's name, Mom and Dad, and even short sentences. Every time he made a statement that people could understand it seemed a glowing energy was released into the room.

What struck me as funny was that, in the midst of all this, people kept telling us to stop what we were doing, that it was hurting him. Every time he'd respond, people would say things like,

"See, he wants you to stop; he doesn't like it. It's hurting him."

It was hard to believe their response in view of the results the process produced. But, that's the way it goes.

The hospital, having had no progress, let me have my way with Bill. When Gene arrived, due to his credentials, the space opened even more. But the doctors were clearly skeptical and so were the nurses. I sensed that their reaction to my believing that aikido had any effect on Bill's state of coma was like believing in Santa Claus, though they were too polite or considerate to say anything.

By the afternoon of the third day when we came to the hospital, Larry Marcus was there. He smiled and said that Bill had responded to him. He smiled when he said that he'd been able to get Bill to talk without having to 'torture' him. Gene and I knew we were on our way home. There was a sense of relief from both of us. It was a very positive sign that Bill was starting to come up into a conscious state on his own. We both began to let ourselves believe things would be okay.

For all of us, there was a strong question about what had happened. I don't know if aikido had really produced results where modern medical technology had no jurisdiction. It might have been easier for Gene to write it off as coincidence, which it may well have been. I might have had a similar problem in reverse, because I wanted it to be true. In retrospect, he describes it as pain and stimulus affecting the reticular activating system causing him to wake up. So, we look at a similar process through different windows.

What it was that really happened there, we'll never know. Would he have woken up if I hadn't come? Was my timing just coincidental? Or is there really some magic in this *aiki* energy flow stuff? It was hard enough for me to believe; so, I can certainly appreciate how hard it must have been for the members of the medical profession. But he had responded. That was clear. And he had responded repeatedly, which did call into question the coincidence theory.

My feeling was that enough internal healing had taken place so that he was ready to be woken up. I believe that the aikido, the pain, the pressure or the *ki* flow itself, had been able to ground his consciousness into contact with the moment, with my voice, and with the rest of us in the room. After repeating that process several times, gradually, he was able to trace his way back into consciousness without help.

I flew home in a dream. This had been the most intensely positive experience I could have possibly hoped for. I had gone on an intuitive impulse without any knowledge of the origin of that guidance. I had gone through with the visit, though some had tried to dissuade me. Because of my willingness to give my life to something I cannot explain, I had possibly touched Bill in a way that brought him back to us. I shudder to think that I almost hadn't gone, because of my fears of the unknown, or of failing, or of looking like an idiot. Without knowing what I was going to do there, I had acted purely and spontaneously out of the larger self.

What happened had been a gift as much to me as to my brother or family. I felt that I had been moved by some knowledge that I did not possess but which possessed me. Now it seems as if there'd never been a choice about going.

Our friend Dickey Ostrin came to see me before I left for the airport. He came up. His eyes were moist. He hugged me as he said goodbye. Then as I was turning to board the plane, he said something that hadn't occurred to me.

He said, "This is the best martial arts story I've ever heard."

Three years later, Bill was alert, active, and had recovered enough of the use of his left side to walk. His voice was almost back to normal. He became involved in computer study, both as therapy and to continue his writing. A previous winner of three National Public Radio documentary awards, he has begun to assemble a new documentary on brain damage.

Now fifteen years later, Bill has completed his masters degree in communication. His video project was submitted for a grant, which he won. He completed a documentary that aired on PBS called, 'When Billy Broke His Head and Other Tales of Wonder.' It received wide acclaim and won The Freedom of Expression Award at Sundance Film Festival and The Columbia Award for Excellence in Broadcasting among many others. Bill also was nominated for an Emmy for writing it. He is working on his next film.

気　気　気

Remembering, Resolving, and Integrating Memories
by
John Luijten - Gen Ki Aikido Yuishinkai - The Netherlands - 3rd Dan

I am 48 years old, live in the southern Netherlands and have practiced aikido for 23 years. For seven years now, I have had my own *dojo*, where I teach kids, teenagers, and adults.

One day, a student of mine asked me if I would be interested in teaching aikido to patients in a private clinic, where they were being treated for mental health problems, such as depression, trauma, burn-out, addiction, panic, and anxiety disorders. I said, "Yes!"

The patients stay at the clinic for approximately seven weeks, and aikido is one of the classes they follow to create a healthy mind in a healthy body. They are divided into four groups ranging from between 10 to 15 people. Twice a month, I teach two groups on Saturday and two groups on Sunday. I never know what the patients are being treated for. In the limited time I have with them, I do not expect to do anything other than to demonstrate how relaxing and positive training can make one feel and to open a door for patients into the world of aikido once their treatment finishes.

In the classes, we practice *ki* exercises, aikido principles and a *hanbo kata*.

During one of the classes when I was teaching the *kata*, a patient started to cry and left the room. After class, she returned and told me the reason for her emotional outburst.

Years ago when she was working in Africa doing missionary work, she witnessed a man being beaten to death with a stick. She blocked this event from her mind, not talking about it or even thinking about it until the lesson with the *hanbo* brought it right back to her. She was surprised by what had happened, as she hadn't thought there was an problem, but her reaction told her otherwise. As a result, she spoke about the incident with her therapists and together with them, she was able to process and deal with this long-buried memory.

After two weeks she asked me to do the *kata* again. This time she stayed on and finished it, as well as the class. She was very happy, because for her it signalled that she had finally come to terms with this terrible trauma.

It had never occurred to her that this event had in fact been deeply affecting her life since that time, yet this simple exercise had opened a window to her subconscious, which enabled her to get her life back on track. It was beautiful to see the relief and joy on her face, and for me it was a wonderful example of why I choose to teach this wonderful art.

As the founder said "True victory is victory over oneself, *masakatsu agatsu*."

気　気　気

Ability, Not Disability
by
**Roisin Pitman - Phoenix (Jersey) School for Therapeutic Arts
5th Dan**

Courage of the Modern Samurai

With the sound of battle a prosaic memory,
The clash of forged steel echoes in eternity,
Samurai forever cast into history,
A faithful, courageous, poetic fraternity.

The samurai of feudal Japan may have been dissolved with the introduction of the Meiji Restoration of 1868, when much of the old order was abandoned in favour of a more equal society for all. But every so often in our modern reincarnation, we find ourselves in the presence of persons who, had they lived several hundred years before, could well have been members of this cultured warrior class. One such modern samurai was my late father, Graeme Ivor Golding Pitman.

As a young child, I was acutely aware of my father's disability. He was totally blind, and I was taught to be extra careful not to leave toys on the floor, once I had finished playing with them, and to extricate myself from a prone position, if he was bearing down on me, unaware of my presence. My father lost his sight in the late 1940s when Britain was recovering from the war, and food rationing was still in existence. Jersey in the Channel Islands, where we are from, had been occupied by the enemy forces and the hardships suffered by the local population were extreme.

The education system in Jersey did not know how to deal with a blind pupil and as a result, my father did not enjoy a good secondary education. However, it did not dull his ambition.

Having gained training through the Royal National Institute for the Blind, and with the courage of some political figures in Jersey, my father trained for a professional qualification, which, he passed with flying colours. This gave him a foot on the ladder of self-determination. Despite his disability, and even with some officials deliberately trying to block his progression, (they believed that people with disabilities should be pitied, rather than encouraged to succeed), he entered the law offices of the Jersey government as a committee secretary.

As a young girl, I noticed that any task he undertook, be it professionally or otherwise, was tackled head-on, with intelligence and skill. He was a positive person who saw his glass as half full rather than half empty. He encouraged me to "look for the ability in the person and not the disability." My personal foundations were built on this positive outlook.

Fast forward to 1990 and history was repeating itself. I found myself on an operating table at Moorfield's Eye Hospital in London, having lost my sight overnight through a dual retinal detachment. After a barrage of tests, it was discovered that I had a rogue gene that caused the collagen in my body to fail to do what it was designed for. In this case, it failed to keep the retinas attached in my eyes and I was prone in the years to follow to suffer from aggravated joints, leading to severe arthritis. It appears that I inherited this from my father, although the condition, Stickler's Syndrome (hereditary progressive arthro-ophthalmology), was not discovered until 1963, more than 16 years after my father became sightless.

Prior to the manifestation of my medical condition, which ultimately put an end to my career as a police officer, I had been a student of aikido for 10 years, starting my own club in September 1987. Many times over that ten-year period, I would often imagine what it would be like to teach aikido to the blind and visually impaired. I spent many hours discussing with my father how he had adapted his life to make the most of his remaining senses. He taught me to understand the elements of touch when sight was not an option, of balance and posture, of spatial awareness, and the ability to internalise thoughts and energy. My father became my teacher, even though he had never practised aikido.

When I lost my sight and woke up in hospital with both eyes covered, I was plunged into a world I didn't know. While I sometimes closed my eyes as a child to try and simulate my father's blindness, it was now real. One's dignity is tested when you have to ask a nurse to help you to the bathroom.

I had many a conversation with the chief surgeon, an Italian *karateka*, who knew that I was a *dan* grade *aikidoka*. He and I stayed up for hours discussing martial arts. As a surgeon he said that he was obliged to inform me that I could no longer practise any type of sport, including aikido, but privately, he said that he knew that it would be impossible to let go and he expected me, against medical advice, to carry on my studies.

When I returned to Jersey, the thought of giving up my aikido studies was banished and I set about re-opening my club. Suddenly, I had to relearn many things, just as my father must have done before me. A small amount of sight returned to my left eye, but none to my right and I had to realign my mind and body to encompass this new situation.

Now I understood, more than ever, the need to adapt the art to the person rather than the other way around. We all learn aikido initially from our first *sensei*; however, as our knowledge increases, we start to fashion our own style of the art best suited to our physical and mental abilities. Our first teacher provides the skeleton while we add the organs and flesh.

Aikido is like an ever flowing river, constantly being energised and refreshed. It should not stagnate or be preserved in aspic. The founder's art was forever changing as his knowledge increased along with his age. His art was adapting to his mind and body, which enabled him to remain powerful and alert even through his later years. This is why aikido is the perfect martial art for the disabled.

A Way to Reconcile the World

My aikido changed to reflect my restrictions in that the movements became more connected both physically and internally, and subsequently became more powerful. It seemed like destiny when I was approached in November 2007 by the mother of a seriously disabled man in his thirties and asked if I would enrol him as an aikido student. I think that she was somewhat taken aback when I accepted him on the spot. I had had some experience of teaching *aiki* based movement therapy to people with Down's syndrome, but this was a huge challenge.

Tyrone Nicholson is a person suffering an acute form of cerebral palsy (quadriplegic athetoid cerebral palsy) that not only affects his motor skills in every limb, but also his speech. He is now wheelchair bound. Ty, as he prefers to be called, is very intelligent and his understanding of aikido is of a high calibre. We had to teach Ty to allow the aikido to 'come to him' rather than try to mould him to any specific way.

Very quickly we found that in addition to the improvement of Ty's abilities on the mat, the practice was starting to shape his life off it, as well. When he first came to us, Ty was at a low point in his life, because although he managed to get work as a messenger at the Jersey General Hospital, his daily life was becoming increasingly difficult. He required a lot of organised health care, and that took away his dignity and independence.

At the aikido club Ty was, and is, his own man, very independent and very much one of the senior students. Admired and respected for who he is, despite his disability, and not because of it. This gave him a new found self-respect that flowed into the rest of his life and he now often describes aikido as 'his life'. His philosophy has always been to 'go for it.'

It is because of Tyrone Nicholson that we have become an all-inclusive aikido club, in which able-bodied and disabled students train side by side. This not only improves the quality of life for differently abled students, it also educates and creates empathy among the more able-bodied members. This is important because typically they would not otherwise come into contact with people who have these problems and aikido has a wonderful way of breaking down those barriers.

Over the years, our program has grown. I am regularly in contact with disabled people who have been touched by the spirit of aikido, whether through the club or through our outreach programme, which brings therapeutic movement to the physically and cerebrally disabled. I have noticed the uplifting feeling that aikido espouses, seeps into their very being, helping to inject hope, energy and a feeling of achievement that is carried forward into their daily lives.

This then rubs off on those around them, whether carers or family, thus helping to create a more harmonious quality of life for all. In Ty's case I have noticed a drastic alleviation in his personal stress levels, both from what he has said to me and from what I have observed in his general demeanour both on and off the mat.

Interacting with Ty has added a new dimension to my studies and teaches me more about the human spirit than I have ever been able to digest during academic study. In many ways, my pupil has become my teacher. We share a unique aikido existence which grows in power and energy as well as transcending the physical aikido to a higher spiritual plane!

気　気　気

Hands and Feet and Heart
by
Katina Bishop - Two Rock - U.S.A. - 4th Kyu

"The glories of the possible are ours." – Bayard Taylor

The *dojo* has a hushed quality in the early morning twilight, and I pause for a moment after removing my shoes to take it in. It's the penultimate day of *kangeiko* training at San Francisco Heart of Aikido, and the *dojo* has added extra early morning classes, so that we have the opportunity to train every day. I am just into my second year of training, and can't believe I've made it through five consecutive days of aikido class. It has taken over my life this week, determined as I am to keep this commitment. By night, I read O Sensei's writings in a bathtub full of Epsom salts, every word reverberating through me, reminding me why I stay on the mat. By day, I spend most of class time focused on which hand goes with which foot, just trying to remember to breathe. Classes this week are especially large and vigorous, and it's a good day when I can follow even half of the class without spinning up into my head.

But today is different. Four small candles are the only light in the room, and our small class moves slowly in the dim light, focused on connection, *musubi*, "tying in" to our partners. A deep feeling of gentleness pervades the room. At one point, I look up to see our *Sensei* practicing a technique with another instructor. Their bodies look like water as they move in perfect sync, like an answer to a problem, the antidote to something stuck. My body relaxes just looking at them, and I turn back to my partner with renewed enthusiasm, moving slowly, listening to where his body naturally wants to go as I move my own. That listening turns to "Wait, do I bring my arm to the left or right now?" almost instantly, but for a moment it is leading us both.

As we bow out, thank each other, and head off the mat, this energy remains, and I soak in it, grateful for the short refuge from the day ahead. I'm reminded of another recent moment of listening near the end of a long journey, a crystallized knowing that it was time for me to leave my job of 10 years. Something solid and good, but not completely right, had to make way for something more unclear, but deeply true. Holding to my decision became easier when, on returning to the organization, I found that sudden changes and the politics that followed meant I no longer felt so at home. Perfect timing, with the exception of one daunting task: working it out with Sara, my boss, mentor and very dear friend.

Sara advocated for me from the moment she started her job as executive director when I was new and very young. She challenged me, collaborated with me, and ate lunch with me nearly every day. She promoted me into positions of leadership, came to my wedding, burst into tears on the street years later when I told her I was ending my marriage.

Although we both knew it would pull me towards a very different life, Sara encouraged me to go on the sabbatical I had earned after a decade of service. She was ready for me to work part-time as I had before, but she had not even considered my leaving.

As we negotiate options, tensions rise. We, who never fight, are fighting, raising our voices, protecting our interests, eating lunch in our offices with the doors closed. I feel a ten-year friendship and creative collaboration heading towards a cliff with no idea of what to do to stop it, and I am coming to work with a tight belly and grim determination just to get through the day.

Today we have another meeting scheduled in the afternoon. I have some good ideas, a solid plan. I know what I want. I just need to spend some time in a café getting my thoughts on paper to prepare. Forty-five minutes after this morning's practice I am standing at the cafe counter waiting for my tea, still enveloped in the mood of the aikido training and looking at an interesting article in the newspaper. It is purely by chance that I glance up and see her.

Sara is picking up her coffee and striding towards the door. In the course of 10 years I have been in many places with Sara, but never in all that time have I run into her unplanned. She's distracted and since I'm off to the side of the room, she hasn't seen me as she heads for her car. I watch her moving towards the door; eyes heavy with a chronic lack of sleep and what seems like sadness. I miss her.

"Sara!"

It comes out of my mouth, loudly, before I can stop it, and she turns on a dime to face me. I feel my breath catch in my throat. I miss her, sure, but I am *not ready* to talk with her, especially with both my career and our friendship on the line. Though she would scoff at the word, Sara's *ki* is very strong. I can feel her all the way across the room as she moves towards me, and I briefly run though my list of options for making a graceful exit with my dignity intact. Then I notice her eyes. The surprise has changed them. The grim determined dullness of the past couple of weeks has given way to something lighter, something I can't quite place, but which I am curious about. She reaches the counter and though each of us is holding complex feelings, we both smile at the strange situation and at each other.

"Do you have a minute?" I ask.

"I'll make one," she answers.

As we head over to a cluster of bar stools I feel it forming, the presence of a cord, sturdy and immovable, stretching between us. It is so palpable I feel as though I could lift my hand and touch it. The two of us sit down and settle. I look at Sara and she looks at me. We remember each other. My careful plans and bullet points are long gone. There is only the cord, and all that it requires. We both have difficult things to say and there is no getting around them. Still, by the time we begin to talk, it's as if a spell has been lifted; within the strength of our connection, a spacious field has opened up, where our hopes and fears can safely land.

I begin, not knowing exactly what words will come out of my mouth, trusting that they will be the right ones. I speak to the changes taking place for me and the conflict between what I want for myself going forward and my commitment and concern for her and for the organization. But the truth of the words is something she can feel through the cord, through my whole being, a solid intention to take care of what matters most to us both.

She is listening to me with all of herself and she responds in kind, talking openly and with feeling, both about her concerns and her real desire to support me. Soon we find that we have shifted into a much more familiar dynamic; one of generosity and trust, of tremendous give and take, of creativity and resourcefulness, one that has characterized all our years of working together. Our grave impasse has become another opportunity to work creatively together. We sit in a focused whirlwind of intense negotiation and brainstorming, trading 'aha' moments, strategizing, even laughing. Finally, when we reach a solid foundation to rest on, I feel the cord releasing us to a more casual level of connection.

One basic action remains the same: I will transition out of my job working with Sara, but every aspect of how it will play out has transformed to meet both of our specific needs. There are still sore spots and glitches to work out, but we have a path forward, a way to approach them. The timetable, the transition plan, the ways in which we will both be supported in the changes, how we will continue to nurture our friendship outside of working together, all have taken a new form. Most importantly, our connection is not only intact, but fundamentally strengthened.

I feel enveloped in stillness during the final day of *kangeiko*, full of gratitude and a sense of awe. I still spin up into my head, and get lost in class and mix up my feet and my hands, but it doesn't bother me in the same way. I have learned deep in my body that regardless of my struggles with technique and grounding and breath, my time on the mat has changed me and it is leaking into my life, shifting its possibilities. I think back to that moment in the café. The aikido training that lives in my body and my heart catalyzed the transformative conversation that Sara and I were able to have together. If that was possible, imagine what else might be within reach, in my own life, in our communities, and in the world at large.

This sense of the larger, of what could be, becomes an imperative for me to do what I can to help bring forth the life and possibility hidden within collision and conflict, connecting us all. It sustains me during the difficult days and lights up the curves on the Path.

気　気　気

A Midnight Challenge

by

Piers Cooke - Coldharbour Aikido Club - England - 7th Dan

I started practicing aikido in February 1982, under Sensei Ken Williams, one of the most influential figures in the UK's aikido history. Ever since then, in social situations, the most common question that I get asked is,

"Have you ever had to use it?"

This is the true story that I tell by way of reply.

I was invited to a surprise party for my brother-in-law's 30th birthday party. I had been practicing aikido for 10 years and had the rank of 3rd *dan*. The party was excellent and my wife and I had completely forgotten about the time and our promise to the babysitter, to be home by midnight.

At 11.40 p.m., we said our goodbyes and with a sandwich in one hand and my sweater over my arm, we walked out of the front door, down a small bank to our car, parked just 60 feet across the road. As I got half way across the road I noticed that there were two people trying to get into the party and that they were just leaning against the front door bell. I stopped in the middle of the road, admittedly a very quiet road, and surveyed the scene.

It took a few seconds for the penny to drop. My first thought was that this seemed like a strange thing for friends to do, especially so late at night. Then I realised that these two were trying to gatecrash the party and that they were pretty drunk. My next thought was that I was probably the best qualified to deal with the situation. So just as the front door opened I said to my sister's best friend,

"It's okay, Tania. I'll deal with this."

I hoped that she would realise what was going on and would go and get some assistance, but instead she said, "Okay," and promptly closed the door. It seemed as if I would have to deal with this on my own.

Having been refused entry, the gatecrashers took umbrage and decided to take it out on me. They both stumbled down the small bank and confronted me in the middle of the road.

Now a description of the participants is required to set the scene. I am about 5' 11" and about 12 stone (168 pounds to those in the U.S.A.). I do not consider myself to be big but I am not small either. The first protagonist was about 6' 3" and I guess about 15 stone (210 pounds), and I think most people would have described him as on the large side. He was partnered by an almost equally large female, though she didn't particularly grab my attention. Both of them were drunk.

So to the confrontation, which started with this opening salvo:

Drunk guy "Who the fuck are you?"

Me "It's my house (it wasn't, but I felt it gave me credibility for stopping their entrance to the party; quick thinking, huh?) "I'm sorry it's a private party you can't go in."

Drunk girl; "Hit him. Hit him." (I promise you that this is what she said.)

There was a stand-off at this point. I could see his mind and body slowly whirring into gear. He was getting ready to hit me with a haymaker of a right.

In my mind I thought the following:

"Okay, Piers. Now's the time to see if this aikido really works. After 10 years of training, you are not backing down."

Then, "Blast, I'm going to have to drop my sandwich and my sweater on the street."

Followed by, "I am going to throw him with an *ikkyo*. He will smash all his front teeth out when he hits the road, but what will be, will be."

My dad was a salesman and he always used to say,

"Make your final pitch, then shut up!'

The first person to speak after that loses. So I repeated,

"I'm sorry it's a private party and you can't go in."

Then I shut up and looked him straight in the eye and I waited for the haymaker that I absolutely felt sure was about to follow, whilst thinking,

"Well now is the test to see if it works!"

Then a very strange thing happened. I could almost hear his mind thinking,

"Why isn't this little guy frightened of me, a big guy?" and slowly through the drunken haze that was his mind, he thought,

"This just isn't right, he must know something that I don't!"

He obviously decided that discretion was the better part of valour, as he chose to turn around, and taking his partner with him, he walked off down the street. I stayed exactly where I was and followed them with my eyes. When they got about 50 yards away, he shouted out at the top of his voice,

"Fucking yuppy!"

And I just thought a very big, "Yes!"

We then got into the car and went home to the baby sitter.

My teacher always used to say that,"The best way to win, is not to have the fight." I felt that on that night I did just that.

So now, when asked if I have had to use aikido for real, I tell this story and let the listener decide.

気 気 気

Mind Leads Body

by

Graham Farquhar - Ki Federation of Great Britain. - England 5th Dan

I first started aikido in June of 1982. My brother Gordon, who is my identical twin, took it up when he began his university studies in the previous October. I agreed to try a class, as my brother was pretty fanatical about it. We had wrestled, scrapped, fought for more than 17 years, and unlike other siblings we were the same height, same weight, and same strength as one another. Neither of us was superior.

In the past when we had fought, there had never been a clear winner, unless one of us dared do some awful deed, which usually resulted in a severe scolding from our mum. To be honest, the fights were brutal; we both saw these occasions as the ultimate challenge.

Albeit that at age 19, we no longer fought as we did, after nine months of Gordon practicing on me, I knew that he was now my better. I would have to be incredibly vicious to outdo him, something that wasn't going to happen. Still, it was good motivation to take up aikido myself.

That first evening, I was introduced to *Ki* Aikido by a highly talented *aikidoka* named Sensei Matt Tennant, an instructor who first studied aikido in 1958 and who was one of the premier aikido teachers in Scotland. At that time, he was a student of Sensei Ken Williams, who remains my teacher to this day.

I learned that it was all about mind and body coordination and how the mind leads the body. I was given a number of examples of how this worked, and I was smitten. I began to practise there, whenever I visited my brother, but in the following year I moved to London. The first thing I did was to find an aikido *dojo*. I tried a number of different *dojos* and styles, Iwama, traditional, affiliated to the Aikikai and also Tomiki, but something was missing! The technical aspects of the training were good, but the "mind" stuff was missing. After a few weeks, I found a *Ki* Aikido *dojo* under the auspices of Sensei Williams and with connection to Koichi Tohei Sensei's organisation. There my practice resumed.

Over the years, I learned so much about the concept of mind moving body. I listened to many stories about it, both on the mat and off, but I always recall being told a particular story about an elderly Japanese woman whose house had caught fire. In this story, the woman had all her worldly goods stored in one incredibly large trunk. Her only thought was to rescue it from the flames. She managed this and then lay down exhausted. She was given some shelter in a neighbour's house, but later when her trunk needed to be moved, two strong, young men were required to lift it. After the event, the old woman couldn't move it at all!

Another tale involved an aikido *shihan*, who was involved in a serious car crash. Somehow, in his efforts to keep the car heading in the appropriate direction, he had bent the steering wheel, by keeping 'unbendable arm', a technique we practice in *Ki* Aikido.

Although I am not certain as to the authenticity of these stories, they served a purpose for me. In each, I saw how body follows mind and therefore, how with mind and body coordinated, almost anything could be achieved.

In 1986, I had just reached second *kyu* and I loved taking *ukemi*. I was physically at my most fit and training three or four times each week. I attended courses and seminars whenever I could. The *ki* aspect was most important in Shin Shin Toitsu. Within the grading system, we had to pass various *ki* tests in addition to the more typical aikido examinations. The first *ki* test is taken alongside fifth *kyu*; the second *ki* test with third *kyu*; and the third *ki* test accompanies first *kyu*, all demonstrating mind and body coordination. As I worked for my first *kyu*, I had no problems with the aikido technique but was struggling with the *ki* test.

Then one Friday night, my teacher invited me to be *uke* and proceeded to throw me through a series of *kokyunage* variations, increasing the power as we continued. It was exhilarating, but I began to feel unwell. Soon I felt very ill, but I didn't want to stop. I kept up a series of strong attacks and my *sensei*, not knowing how I was feeling, kept going. All I could think was, "Don't be sick on the mat; whatever you do, don't throw up on the mat." When we finished class, I bowed out and raced to the toilets where I vomited violently.

Over the weekend, I got steadily weaker and more ill and was finding it harder to get to bed. The following Monday, I decided to go to the doctor. Her news rocked me. She told me that I was seriously anaemic and that she needed to take some blood samples, because she thought that I might have ulcerative colitis, an inflammatory disease that attacks the colon. Nowadays, when events like this happen, we all use the internet to understand what is going on, but this was before that, so I had to digest what I could from the doctor. She told me that I might need to take steroids and advised me to go home and rest. In the afternoon, I received a telephone call from her; I had a case of ulcerative colitis. She was coming round to see me, and an ambulance would be there within an hour to take me to the hospital. What?? This could not be true. Only three days ago I was taking *ukemi* from my teacher and had been engaged in such vigorous practice with my *sempai*. Surely, I was not that ill?

I was admitted to hospital and underwent test after test. I received an immediate blood transfusion, supplementary fluids, and steroids, but I wasn't getting any better. Four days later, the physicians told me that I needed to be seen by the surgeons. Tests had shown that my colitis was so bad that I had what was called 'toxic megacolon.' My colon had swollen to over twice its normal size and was likely to rupture at any moment. They needed to operate and remove it. I would be left with a medical appliance called an ileostomy, a bag attached to the side of my torso that would collect faeces. Furthermore, there was a risk that during surgery, my colon could rupture and that would be very serious indeed, as all of the poisonous faecal matter spilling from within the colon could contaminate the abdominal cavity and thereby also result in long-term illness.

The message was delivered sympathetically, but it came as such a blow. My first thoughts were, "How can I train? How could I take *ukemi* with a bag?" I was completely devastated! But I knew I could do this and that all I needed to do was get through the surgery. I told myself that whilst my body might be in a bit of shambles, mind leads body, and so I could get through this.

The next day, I awoke in intensive care. There was a cut from my breastbone to my pubic bone, and I was suffering. Even with pain relief medication, my body hurt a lot. The surgeon explained why. He told me that my abdominal muscles had been well-developed and that they had to be cut for the surgery and then sown back together. As a result of this, these muscles had effectively become shorter. I realised the full consequence of this a week later when I could once again stand up. I was a full four inches shorter than my twin brother. I was bent over like an octogenarian and shuffling around, but I had made it. There was also good news. My ileostomy was probably not permanent; and if they could reverse it, there would be no need for an ileostomy bag.

I recovered as quickly as I got ill, and after three months, I ventured onto the mat once more. I spoke to my teacher, *Sensei* Williams, about my forthcoming operation.

He looked at me, smiled and said "Think of the forthcoming surgery as your third *ki* test, one that is about your mind and not so much your body."

So in due course, I went back to hospital to reverse the ileostomy, but it was not a success. I became ill again and was required to consult with a specialist surgeon by the name of Professor Norman Williams. He was one of few who could perform an operation, wherein they use the small intestine to make a small reservoir called a 'w-pouch.' This would act as my colon, albeit in a slightly different way.

It didn't start off well. I was transferred to the hospital having developed septicaemia. This meant that toxins from severe bacterial infection had spread throughout the whole body to poison my blood. Yet again, I found myself in a hospital bed, but after ten days, my condition stabilised and I was able to undergo surgery. The first part of the procedure was to form the pouch which would again result in a temporary ileostomy. No problem, I had been there and done that.

Initially, the surgery appeared to have been a success, but then there was another unexpected complication. I seemed to have real pain in my shoulders and then in my chest. This was diagnosed as deep vein thromboses. Apparently, blood clots in my legs had moved to my lungs. I had to have drugs to thin my blood in order to stop the clots moving to my brain, which would have resulted in a stroke. I had thought that all would be well after that near miss, but then I started to run a fever, a very high fever. After about four days, the Professor came to see me. He had bad news. They had found an abscess in my newly created pouch and there was some internal bleeding. He had to juggle between trying to stop the internal bleeding, which is normally done by clotting the blood and trying to reduce the clotting in my lungs. It was a 'Catch-22' scenario.

We persevered, but after a week of this balancing act I was getting worse. I became delirious and lost all sense of reality with the drugs and the fever. I have no recollection of the next five days. The Professor spoke with me during one of my lucid moments. He said he believed he had to operate that evening, as he was concerned for my life. I had been running a temperature of more than 40C for five days now, and he had to do something about it. He would have to take out my pouch and leave me with a permanent ileostomy. My hopes of normal life were dashed. We had a discussion. I had now been in his care for five weeks and we had developed a good honest relationship. I asked, probably pleaded, with him, to give me 24 hours, as I was sure this could be turned around.

"Just give me another 24 hours, and if my temperature is still above 40C, I will sign the consent papers."

The Professor was wary. He said that he couldn't give me 24 hours. It was too long and he wouldn't risk my life, but he would give me until the next morning's 8.00 a.m. ward round.

That night, all I could think was that I would beat this. It would not beat me. I thought of the story of the elderly Japanese woman and her trunk and said to myself, "Come on! This is why you train in mind and body coordination." I remembered *Sensei*'s words,

"This could be your third *ki* test."

Well here I was, positioned with mind and body coordinated and waiting for the test to come. Remember, "Mind controls body; mind controls body."

I fell asleep thinking, "Just lower my temperature; just get it down."

I woke the next morning with the day nurse just coming on duty. Her first duty was to check my pulse, blood pressure, and temperature. She looked at me and re-took my temperature. It was 37 degrees. The Professor came round 30 minutes later. He couldn't believe it. He was amazed and very pleased. Yep, my temperature was down and it was staying down. He cancelled my operation, which had been scheduled for 9.00 a.m. that morning. I had done it; I had passed the third *ki* test. To me, those five years of training had come together. That's why I had been studying *Ki* Aikido. I had managed to put aikido into my daily life, which is exactly what Tohei *Sensei* said the practice was intended for.

And so, 20-plus years later, where am I? I am continuing my study and practice of aikido and I am with the same teacher who told me all those years ago to treat a very real challenge as a *ki* test. All the surgery I have undergone has not diminished my enthusiasm for the art of aikido. There has, however, been one peculiar side effect. The result of all the surgery has been that I have a very noisy gut, which has a habit of making the loudest gurgling sounds at the most inappropriate moments. On the mat, sitting in *seiza* before class tends to be when it decides to be the loudest. Over the years, I have got used to my fellow *aikidoka* looking around to see what on earth could have made such a sound and then asking incredulously,

"Was that you?"

So, if you are ever sitting in *seiza* at a seminar and you suddenly hear a gurgling sound, you will know that's me!

Aikido Works
by
Reesa Abrams - Aikido of Santa Cruz - U.S.A. - 5th Kyu

Today, March 17, 2009, I have a 10:30 am appointment at Lu Lu Carpenter's coffee shop by the Museum of Art and History on Cooper Street in Santa Cruz and I am waiting outside for the person I have agreed to meet. I am dressed up for a meeting later in the day and so I do not look like a local.

Out of the corner of my eye I notice a homeless man stalking around the outside seating area about 10-12 feet away. His expression is very intense, like he is making a decision to do something. He is Caucasian, 30 to 40 years old, about 5'9" tall, approximately 150 pounds, light brown hair messy to his ears, wearing a greenish tan or grey shirt, trousers, and a long rain coat. He is carrying a grey backpack and a sleeping bag. The man is not drunk, but there is something not quite right about him.

I feel him eying me and it makes me feel uncomfortable. The only thing significant about me compared to the other café patrons is that I am dressed up. I am also on the end of the open area; so, my bag is the easiest to go for and offers the best chance to get away. I think to myself that if he can get hold of my bag, he can escape behind the building across the street and disappear in a maze of alley ways.

My sixth sense is working overtime and then all at once I can see that the man has made a decision and so have I. I am not going to stay here to find out what he is up to. My best option is to head for the door of NextSpace, which is where I have to run an errand in any event and it's only five doors down across the street. He is actually closer to my destination than I am, but I am confident that by taking a lead that I have time on my side.

I walk briskly and head directly toward the door with my entry key in my hand. I know that all I have to do is pass the key fob over the lock mechanism and the door will open immediately. He is pursuing me and I can feel his energy, but I make my way to the door and I pass the key over the electronic eye, grab the door in my left hand, and do a quick two-step turn, which allows me to just slip in and slam the door. I am just in time and watch him as he arrives at the door with an angry frown on his face. He looks at me and slams his hand hard on the door window!

I rush up stairs and tell the CEO, what has just happened and he has me call the police. When I give them my report the officer asked me how I knew to be aware and to be so conscious. So, I tell him that Linda Holiday Sensei is my mentor at Aikido of Santa Cruz. He says that he is glad to hear that. He remarks that he has heard good things about how participation at Aikido of Santa Cruz seems to have had beneficial effects in other such incidents around town.

This is only the beginning of the third week of returning to aikido after over three years of not practicing on the mat, but after speaking to the cops, my spouse, and Sensei, I am certain that my return was a very good decision.

Center.

Breathe.

Domo arigato gozaimashita (thank you very much) to all my sensei.

気　気　気

A Peaceful Encounter
by
Bjorn Saw - Aikido Alive London - England - 5th Dan

Walking home late at night in central Stockholm I pass through an unlit passage in a small park. It's quite late and there are not many people about. The subway system has closed for the night and I need to find the night buses to take me to the suburbs.

I am feeling good, relaxed and enjoying my walk through the quiet city. I value such times alone, as it allows me time to reflect and to drop or fall into myself. I become very quiet inside, absorbed and totally at peace. (This is also what I value in aikido; a peaceful mind and a balanced body).

A Way to Reconcile the World

As I am walking through the park, I see a group of youngsters hanging around off the pathway further ahead. I become aware that I have left the part of the park that is lit and suddenly there are no other people around. In my peaceful state of mind, I take it all in and proceed without any tension. Then one of the young men steps out. Still a fair distance from me, he puts his hand in his pocket and turns towards me.

Now I have never been in a fight or been threatened before, and I had no experience of a really dangerous situation, so what happened next was revealing and truly significant to me.

He puts his hand in his coat pocket as if grabbing something. He swiftly looks me up and down, and I can see him take in his surroundings to see if anyone else is near. Suddenly, I am acutely aware of danger. It is like an alarm bell and flashing lights have gone off. Despite this, I feel unaffected and surprisingly cool. I just ease my hands out of my pockets and continue walking, letting everything unfold before my eyes.

I realize that this heightened sense of danger doesn't stem from my own fear and actually doesn't have anything to do with me at all. It is the situation itself that evokes this feeling. The warning bells started to ring the moment the young man turned toward me. His intent created this highly charged situation that we both experienced and equally shared. But there was no fear and I remain calm and feel like an onlooker witnessing the event. As he feels the tension too, he sees my lack of reaction and he hesitates. He surrenders his intent, takes his hand out of his pocket and turns back to his friends. As fast as it had come, the feeling disappears and normality resumes.

I continue walking as if nothing had happened, relaxed and truly enjoying the moment. Not because I was happy to have escaped a possible dangerous encounter, but that the whole event has shown me how impersonal a genuinely hostile situation can be. If I had responded in kind to what I had felt from this young man, it would have been natural to respond with fear or anger and then the chance of violence would have been so much greater.

Through aikido we learn to recognize our habitual reactive defence mechanisms in order to transform our relationship with, and our response to them, so that in the end we will be able to see things as they are and respond appropriately.

When the spirit of an event overtakes us, we come to see that we share and partake in the same experience. In aikido we sometimes call this *musubi* (tying our *ki* together). By treating the experience that night as just that, rather than a personal attack, the threat was never realised and the aggression dissipated naturally. Through this union hostility ceases of its own accord.

気　気　気

The Lawyer's Tale
by
Frank Bloksberg - Aikido'Ka - U.S.A. - 3rd Dan

This story is about a high-stakes lawsuit involving my horribly injured client and a multinational corporation. You know the company. Everyone does. The results could mean financial independence forever for my client, in other words, big money. With virtually unlimited resources, the company resisted mightily. My client had just me upon whom to depend for advocacy.

The company hired a leading defense law firm. One of that firm's most experienced partners lead the team. Let's call him George (not his real name). George led the six to ten professionals assigned to the case.

The case had proceeded slowly over years and so I knew George pretty well by now. George was a highly skilled attorney, and he would do pretty much anything to win, including lying and cheating. He also considered himself highly ethical.

By this point, I had grown really sick of George's shenanigans. His deviousness and ruthlessness were wasting tons of time, money and, worse yet, his techniques were proving effective. While the lawsuit was going well for my client, things could change very, very quickly.

Sometimes, the judge fell for George's tricks. I needed to do something, but I didn't know what.

I considered my aikido training. George was an *uke* who felt he could do most anything and he was right. When dealing with difficult *ukes*, I knew that *atemi* worked well in gaining cooperation.

One day, George called. We discussed a particular aspect of the case that we planned to soon argue in court. George was his usual self. By that, I mean that he kept lying about every little thing; the facts, my arguments, his arguments, the time of day. You get the picture. The time for *atemi waza* had arrived.

(I have loosely paraphrased the conversations from what actually happened.)

Me George, you know what you said isn't true. Please tell the truth.

George Of course it's true! You're arguing that the moon is made of cheese. Since you can't prove the moon is made of cheese, you're going to lose!

Me Have you lost your mind? I never argued anything of the sort. I understand that you think lying to the judge might work. But you can't possibly imagine that I would be convinced or swayed by your lies about what I have said.

George You made the moon-cheese argument and now you're stuck with it.

Me George, you're a deeply religious man, aren't you?

George Yes.

Me Do you take the ethical teachings of your religion seriously?

George Yes. My religion and its ethical teachings are about the most important things in my life.

Me OK, then. Do you lie to your wife and children to get what you want?

George (*In an irritated tone of voice*) Of course not! I am completely truthful with them.

Me Do you teach your children that lying is good if it gets them what they want?

George (*George is obviously getting mad*). Of course not! I teach them that lying is wrong.

Me When you put your head on your pillow at night and contemplate how you've behaved through the day, do you congratulate yourself for being a liar and a hypocrite?

George What?! (*George is hopping mad now.*)

Me You understand what I am saying to you, George. You claim to be deeply religious, following ethics that are incredibly important to you. But, you're not living up to your supposed ethics, George. You lie to me and to the judge constantly. You're a liar and a hypocrite. Knock it off.

George (*In a furious tone of voice*) That is the most unprofessional thing I've ever heard! You are completely out of line!

Me Actually, I think this is the most professional conversation you've ever experienced. It's time for you to conduct yourself honorably and ethically. George hung up on me.

I didn't hear from George for a couple of weeks. That felt like quite a long time, because the case was active and we had a lot of things to discuss.

And then the phone rang. The caller I.D. told me George was calling.

Me Good afternoon.

George (*In a soft, meek voice*) Frank?

Me Yes, George. What can I do for you?

A long silence.

George (*Continuing in an unusually soft voice*) You were right. It will never happen again.

Me I believe you, George.

George I'll talk to you later.

And with that, I knew the case would ultimately settle.

George was good to his word and never lied to me or to the judge again.

気　気　気

Lifted
by
Marill Poole - Beaconsfield Dojo - England - 6th Dan

I would never have thought of taking up a martial art. It just never entered my head until I went to a self-defence class. Having grown up with three brothers, I was a bit feisty and found that actually, aikido was right up my street. In fact, I enjoyed it so much that when the course ended I was heartbroken. Jack Poole, who happened to be my teacher, asked me to take up aikido but I said, "No" initially, as I felt the practitioners were too serious. I just wanted to have fun and let off a bit of steam.

However, it was not long before I felt a strong pull to explore aikido. At first, I didn't appreciate that it was anything more than a self-defence system, but it was not long before I began to see that it offered far more than that. It was, in fact, a philosophy for life. Before I knew it, I was hooked. I needed to have something in my life that I could go on practicing and learning for as long as my body would allow. Aikido was absolutely the answer.

To that end marrying the instructor, Jack, was a good plan. I had no end of training and it also made the classes more affordable. My aim was to catch up with his knowledge, but inevitably as I climbed the knowledge ladder, so did he. So, he remained several rungs ahead of me. He seemed to treat me harder than he did the others and I approached him about this. His explanation was that I was a woman in what is predominantly a man's world and he wanted to show that there is no gender in aikido. We are all *aikidoka* and therefore equal, as we are not reliant upon strength, but on using the principles that sit at the heart of aikido. Strength has a limit but power is limitless.

What I didn't know at the time was that aikido was to play a major part in my life and also shape my career. I trained professionally as a nurse, but unfortunately I lost my kidney and spleen, as a result of picking up an infection, and therefore, had to give up nursing.

Needless to say, I was heartbroken, but then I remembered that the British Aikido Board strongly recommended that potential aikido coaches should have first aid training. As a result, I attended a First Aid at Work (FAW) course. I suddenly realised that this was a way back into the clinical world, and set about becoming a FAW trainer. Once established as a commercial trainer for St John Ambulance, I soon found a module called 'Manual Handling,' which was to re-direct my life again and bring me closer to aikido. I could instantly see the correlation between what was being taught in this module and what I had learnt on the mat.

The challenge was to convince staff that they would benefit from understanding aikido principles. At the beginning, they mostly switched off as soon as I mentioned martial arts. They couldn't relate to it and so they stopped listening. I knew I had to find a different way of approaching the subject and so I became a Pilates teacher and a tai chi practitioner.

It was like flicking a switch, because as soon as I told them this, they became much more interested in what I had to say. They knew enough to know that Pilates was something to do with working core muscles, and recognised tai chi as something to do with groups of old people exercising in a park.

My way of introducing aikido was to explain to staff that when I became a Pilates teacher I had to do a demonstration. I was the oldest in the class and could not do half the exercises that the younger students could do, because they had youth and age behind them. But I had noticed that each time they prepared their core muscles to carry out whichever exercise they chose to do, they had experienced no challenging interference.

I suspected that if they had to do the same thing under pressure, their skill levels would drop dramatically. To that end I designed several challenging exercises that proved my point. Then I demonstrated that I could maintain my skill level, even when confronted with complexity and challenge. I told them this was because of my aikido training. When they saw this they respected me much more as a teacher.

The medical staff attending my courses could suddenly understand why it was so important to take on board what I had to offer, as they had to maintain their skill levels in highly pressurised situations.

It is quite a challenge to find ways of passing on what I have learnt on the mat to staff that do not have the years of concentrated training and exploration of technique that an aikido student does. With constant and regular practice comes muscle memory and this is not something that can easily be attained by hospital staff, who only get a four-hour training session every year or so. Despite this, they are expected to perform at high levels even in very complex situations. To me, it's like asking beginners to do techniques at *dan* grade level on their first night.

It took me years to find ways of dealing with this, but in the end I found that by using visualisation techniques, trainees could re-produce the correct body mechanics to perform their tasks competently. This was something I learned through my own aikido training.

I remember Jack explaining things to me in picture language. To help me remember a picture or feeling, he once placed *zori* under my arms and I had to ensure that they did not fall. This had the effect that I would use my body rather than my arms separately. This particular idea, I have been able to use, because whilst it may not give learners an in-depth understanding of the mechanics of lifting, they are able to feel what it's like to lift in this posture. So very quickly they are able to do it right and to do it now.

I say to my National Health Service staff that they must become like Olympic weight lifters, in that they must practice their routine of movement every day and build their future on the muscle memory they develop daily. This is vital, because there is a very fine margin between right and wrong when it comes to the use of power and strength. The long-term health of care providers, and indeed the well-being of their patients, is at stake.

For my part, this exploration of training people in such circumstances off the mat, has forced me to develop new training strategies, which I have been able to use on the mat as well, which has been an unexpected gift.

Every day I learn!

気　気　気

Tales from a Bouncer
by
Tim Bamford - Test Valley Dojo - England - 1st Dan

I started training in aikido when I was 12 years old and I have had various reasons to use both the principles and techniques in different real life situations.

As I am a door supervisor, I deal with open aggression nearly every weekend. I would like to offer a few examples whereby the physical confrontations have been avoided simply by adopting the sort of positive and harmonious mindset that I have learnt on the mat and which in my opinion is so crucial to this martial art.

There have also been a few instances when I have had to use aikido in a physical way, but even then, it has always enabled me to deal with the situation in a non aggressive way.

Being confident in your ability is often one of the main ways in which trouble can be avoided. The less you look like a victim, the more likely it is that people will leave you alone, and aikido helps this because it encourages good posture, awareness and correct positioning.

A Way to Reconcile the World

When dealing with abusive and outwardly aggressive patrons, I have found that just standing with confidence and in our standard or 'defensive' stance deters all but the most determined aggressors.

On the rare occasion where something more is required, it is important to stay calm, as having someone square up to you is always daunting. On one occasion, we refused entry to a customer because he had been giving other colleagues grief. It was my job to tell him this and when I did, he proceeded to back away and rip off his shirt, becoming ever more abusive. He beckoned me to join him in the street. Placing myself in front of him, I took the standard aikido *hanmi* stance, hands relaxed by my side, posture tall and confident, face calm, while projecting intent as we do on the mat. He then promptly picked up his shirt, put it back on, shook my hand, apologised and walked out of town. Fantastic! There have been many occasions when I have managed to carry out my job successfully in this way.

Because we practice on the mat, the techniques we use are fluid and we get used to throwing our partner, only to see them bounce back up and come at us again. In the real world rolling on the pavement is not quite so easy, especially for those who are not trained. By way of example, once I was attacked by a man in a bar, who attempted to lunge forward with a bottle in a passable seventh form attack. Now *kotegeishi* is a brilliant way to defend oneself on such an occasion. If nothing else, it trains us to move out of the way, which is definitely a good idea. In this instance the man hit the floor with a bang and ended up with his feet up in the air, winded. I was then able to disarm him with ease. I found the results surprisingly spectacular.

Once or twice I have found myself in a *randori* sort of situation, but for real. On the mat, it is perhaps one of the most intense and realistic exercises that we undertake, but without truly putting ourselves on the line. I don't advise anyone to put themselves in a situation, in which they have to try out their technique for real, but I can say that generally in these situations, the assailants do not roll smoothly and they do not attack in a coordinated way.

One night I knocked into someone, simply because he was pushed back into me by his friends and consequently he spilt his drink, a common occurrence. This man blamed me, became extremely irate and then was joined by two of his mates. I took control by placing myself where I would not be surrounded and where I was able to move. As the first attack came, it was actually a very simple thing to redirect the gentleman concerned into his compatriots, which meant that they had no opportunity to attack. In fact the only successful blows that were exchanged were amongst themselves. Where the opportunity arose I placed them on the ground. When I did, they did not get up very quickly.

In general, I have found that aikido works in everyday life as well. It seems to have a positive impact on the people around me. The more positive and happy I am, the more positive and happy they are. It may seem strange, but perhaps the thing that has made the most difference in my job has not been the technique that I have learnt, but rather a set of principles and state of mind, which when applied correctly usually means that bad situations never arise in the first place.

気　気　気

To Hell and Back Again
by
Mike Forde - Association of Ki Aikido - England - 1st Dan

I had always been good at sports. I was also highly intelligent, having an I.Q. once measured at upwards of 140, which I suppose made me precocious as a child. At an early age (about five or six years old) I was taught basic judo and how to box. I never forgot the basic judo throws, but I never went further with it. I did, however, box and I was good at it. By my 12th birthday I fought for my school. I also took up gymnastics, which I also loved and for which I won lots of prizes. I liked nothing better than circuit training and commando type assault courses; all of these I took to like a duck to water.

The other side of having the fighting background and a fighting mind was that it did get me into trouble as a kid. I had a bad temper (and ginger hair) and I wasn't really able to handle it. So, I got into lots of scrapes. At 17, I even received an offer to become a professional boxer, but Mum said, "No." She said, "I want a son for a son, not a cabbage." That stuck with me and I obeyed her wishes.

Instead, I became a bit of a hippy, going to music festivals, dabbling in drugs, though I never quite managed the peace and love bit. It was during this time that the troubles in Ireland began to kick off, and having an Irish Catholic background myself, I took a keen interest. I felt this very personally and wanted to help. For the first time, I studied Irish history instead of being instructed in it by my Irish relatives, and my eyes were opened. I had heard of the 'Black and Tans' and the terror they brought to our Irish villages. My mother told me many tales of atrocities by 'them' on 'us.' But I was born in England, and it was up to me to draw my own conclusions dispassionately and intellectually, without bias. The end result was that I joined the British Army.

My peculiar talents did not go long un-noticed and I was soon placed on a course, which I shall call 'Logistics, Signals and Intelligence (LSI for short).' I am not able to discuss this even now, but suffice it to say that I found my niche. I loved it. It was a demanding course lasting nearly two years. Morning, noon, and night, I slept, ate, and lived it. The LSI training would alter my perceptions massively, and give me a deep insight into the 'Troubles' in a way I could not have thought possible.

The nature of my service meant that I experienced horrifying events that, whilst I did not realise it at the time, left me terribly scarred. Below is an example of the sort of thing I mean. It is disturbing and not for the faint of heart, but this was my reality.

02.30 hours. January 1971 - I am dressed in a thermal suit as is the rest of my unit. I am very cold, but at least I am not freezing. A fibre optic telescope is raised from the five-foot by three-foot by six-foot-long natural cut in the land. Camouflaged and unseen, I've been here with my colleagues on observation-only duty for five days. "Snap." We all hear the twigs go and turn our optics in that direction. We see a man raising his sten gun. It's him or us. "Thud-thud." ....the sound of silenced death. His brains are spattered for 20 meters in all directions. He dies before he can shoot. I think then that this mother's son might at least get a funeral. Had it been my own death, my mother would never get the chance to smile or cry at my grave. I would be anonymously dispatched in an unmarked grave.

In 1976, I left the army and four years later attended a reunion in Hereford. There are lots of gaps where brothers once stood. There'd been many more battles, many more bodies, not only in Northern Ireland, but also in Yemen and Oman. I don't grieve, that's not how we think of them or of ourselves. It's part of the job.

"Well done, soldier. You're a credit to your unit and to yourself." I was bloody well good and I knew it.

Then I went silent.

Who could I talk to? Seven jobs in a year, and the blackness became solid and smothering. I knew I was dying inside. No fear, just wistful, or so I thought. The psychiatrist told me the tears and the bad dreams would pass. They didn't. So now, who could I trust when they'd all left me to it? No support, no comrades, no anything you would call normal. Just black nights and red tempers.

"Fuck with me and I'll tear your face off,", and I nearly did so many times.

I didn't think that I had injured the last one, but then I heard about his broken arms and fractured, lucky skull. He lived and I was dying, with the booze and methamphetamines being my only friends. I needed those mission-issue white tablets. They made me forget and released the silence inside.

April 1999 - My Mum died! "Goodbye Mother, I love you".

November 1999 - I am sitting on a bag and it all comes flooding back. I cried for the first time in as long as I can remember. The sobs racked my skinny body and I asked Mum,

"What can I do that would've made you proud of me and proud in me?"

The thought came unbidden. "Aikido." That was all the thought said. I was puzzled and a little spooked. But a similarly powerful experience in 1992 when a voice in my head said,

"Will you sacrifice it all for this drink?"

I hadn't drunk since and I never missed it.

So where had that come from? From Mum? From me? I don't know now, any more than I did then, but I followed up. Good soldiers do that.

I found a club and I joined.

Charles Harris was my teacher and he was plain speaking and totally honest. His attitude was one of total acceptance, even if I disliked something or didn't agree. He literally and metaphorically put himself in my place and in that way we were able to work together. When practising, I found myself, more often than not, hitting the floor and wondering how I got there. I attempted to punch him at his request. Time slowed almost to nothing. There was a sense of floating, a pleasant feeling. I looked up at him thinking, "What happened?" No pain, no fear, just sheer amazement. From that point, Aikido, I was yours and you were mine.

My training was not without problems, as it turned out that I had contracted Hepatitis C. For two years, I was so tired that on some days I couldn't walk. On others, I couldn't eat, but I trained when I could. Slowly but surely, I progressed and made my way through the grades.

I received my red belt (fifth k*yu*) in February of 2000. That meant I could break fall safely and could perform the first lock hold well enough and safely enough to protect myself and my *uke* from injury. Because I tended to rely on strength over technique, I often hurt either myself or my *uke*, but I thought I was good. At that point, I was invited to attend my first out-of-town seminar in Margate and was to meet the head *sensei* of our organisation, David Currie. I had heard his name mentioned and the general comments seemed to be that this guy was different. Descriptions ranged from 'unbelievable,' to 'a different order of human being.'

As the 'thousand-yard stare man,' or soldier, I did think "Oh yeah?", but I went along for the ride.

So, there I was in Margate, along with many others from the British *Ki* Aikido Association, on a Friday evening in January. We met up at a local seaside pub that evening. People had come from all over the country and we all had a common cause. We were all *aikidoka*. It was an unforgettable experience. There were doctors, lawyers, bricklayers and other ex-army personnel. There were security experts, dancers and all sorts of movers and shakers. It was an eclectic group of people together in one place, which would spark the imagination of any good scriptwriter. The gathering itself was amazing, but the best was yet to come.

I met David Currie *Sensei*. He carried himself with a sort of calm and inner-peacefulness that I thought only mystics or dead people possessed. On the mat and I found myself training with an ex-marine called Ryan. He and I formed an almost instant bond, both being ex-servicemen. Although we liked each other a lot, he irritated me. He was so damned good at what he did that I felt rubbish beside him. I recall my happiest moment was when, in the heat of the moment and having forgotten the instructions given, Ryan galloped towards me in what was meant to be a full-on attack. I went into 'close quarter combat' mode. I grabbed his lapels, twisted my legs under his belt-level, and launched him six feet into the air, sending him flying in the direction he had been travelling.

Normally, if I had done that to anyone else, it would have finished the thing off right then and there. But what did Ryan do? After being projected about 20 feet over my six-foot high head, he touched down on the mat and simply rolled out of the fall. He turned toward me then, just smiled, and said "That wasn't aikido."

I replied, "No, but it worked!"

We both thought that was very funny, but I was a bit uneasy. How had he done that? The throw I performed would have taken out an ordinary person, ergo, Ryan was not 'any ordinary person,' and I just couldn't figure it out.

A Way to Reconcile the World

David Currie (DC) Sensei came onto the mat next and demonstrated a *kaitenage* technique from a knife attack. His *uke* was duly sent cart wheeling along on the same path of his initial attack, minus his weapon and very much minus his dignity.

It was so quick that I missed the foot movements that accompanied the technique. So DC said,

"Okay. I'm going to slow this right down, so that you can see the foot movements properly."

I stared intently at his feet as he repeated the technique. Here it comes, then it's over. I am staring at his feet, really concentrating, but somehow the technique is complete and I am still none the wiser. He does the thing for a third time, very slowly, but despite my best efforts, I just don't understand what happened. Did his feet move? It wasn't only odd; it was downright weird. Who was this man? I started to understand what was meant by 'another planet' and 'unbelievable.' Both descriptions applied, and still do to this day. I was truly hooked.

"I want to be able to do that," I thought.

Not long after that first seminar, I earned my yellow belt. Some might say that this is their proudest moment, along with getting a black belt. For me though, it was an achievement I was proud of, but not half as much as my pride in getting my orange belt a year later in 2001.

By then, I was six months into my treatment for Hepatitis C and sometimes the prescription medications made me so weak I couldn't walk. They took a heavy toll, but I never stopped believing in aikido.

I had not yet noticed how the art had begun to change me in ways I would not realise for some long time ahead. It was probably obvious to Charles *Sensei* that I was changing, but I was too sick to know or care.

At my orange belt test, my *uke* really went for it. I knew I was doing well, because at first he just looked amazed, then amused, then very respectful, because he knew how hard I was trying just to keep standing. During this, I used *kiai* for the first time. This not only surprised him but amazed me, as it just seemed to energise me. The sound bounced around the *dojo* and I was left wondering whether this energy was coming *from* me or *through* me.

At that particular grading, I met a man called Philippe Gerard, with whom I was to study weapons and work with for all of my gradings from third to first *kyu*, and then beyond this to first and second *dan*. Philippe had been a student of David Currie Sensei and was the most innovative, motivating person in aikido that I had met. His knowledge and instruction in weapons was why I chose to study with him. I needed the extra training and he gave it to me in spades. Suffice to say that at my green belt grading Philippe's input ensured my weapons work was excellent.

Green belt (third *kyu*) was the one that I had said I would earn for Mum and then stop. I had a distinct idea of what I wanted to do, as I had witnessed a green belt grading by a man called Jens when I was a beginner. He was a very tall man, well over six feet tall and big in all dimensions. His hands were like shovels on the end of long arms. He had a huge head and an even bigger smile. He performed *ikkyo* on me and it felt so odd, like syrup flowing over my arm as I was brought to the floor. No pain, no nothing really, and whilst physically it was very gentle, there was immense power. He didn't move so much as flow. This was the kind of green belt I really wanted to be able to demonstrate. If I could do what he did, the way he showed me, I felt that I would have reached perfection and I wouldn't need to seek further.

I passed, but was no 'Jens' and never would be. I would always be me and could never be him. When I came home that evening after receiving my belt, I held it in the air and said out loud,

"Mum, this is for you. I did it!"

Then the tears came. Deep sobs, my body shaking and racked. I could not stop the tears from flowing, just as they are now, whilst writing this.

I had put all my Mum's photos away when she died. I had never spoken her name, nor would anyone who knew me. Her death affected me deeply, but I had buried my grief. Now, it all came out.

"Mum, I'm so sorry I put you in that drawer, but the pain was too much. I couldn't face it."

I took her photo out and looked at her image for the first time in more than three years. I smiled as I saw my best friend. I smiled at her photos as I set them in a place of honour, where they have been ever since. It turned out that my green belt was not just for Mum but very much for me, as it had an obviously huge cathartic effect on me too.

I knew then that she would want me to go on until I could go on no longer. Blue, brown, black, here I come and it's for *me* now. It took a year for blue belt. It was very hard and nearly drove me mad with frustration, but I got it.

Then it was time to go for my brown belt (first *kyu*) Something odd happened, one of those strange ethereal experiences. Very Zen.

I was facing Mike, a *tanto* in his hand held at the knot in my belt. Behind me Ian held a *tanto* to my back. The ideal response is to deal with both attackers quickly and in such a way as to avoid any injury. I cannot quite say why but I froze. Then Ian pushed his *tanto* into my spine ever so slightly and everything went sort of fluid. Space was no longer there. All sound stopped and things no longer existed. It was as if there was a bubble around me. I could hear nothing and I wasn't looking or seeing in any way I could explain to you. There was no hurry at all. I had just felt this point in my back. I don't know what I did, but the next thing I knew both Ian and Mike were on the floor looking surprised. My mind snapped back (and I mean 'snapped' because that is what happened) and I was back in real time.

I am told it was one of the best brown belt gradings Charles *Sensei* had seen. Personally, I don't remember much more than stated. Everything seemed like a dream, but the award of first *kyu* at the end of it, really spoke for itself. I knew I had taken a significant step towards a different level of understanding, but I didn't appreciate exactly where I had arrived.

Sometime later, I was sitting down at the edge of the *dojo* and watching another student training for his green belt. He said to Charles,

"I'm too knackered. I can't go on tonight."

From somewhere came this deep, powerful voice. With absolute authority and absolute assurance, it says,

"No, Dave, don't do that! This is the moment you <u>can</u> go on. You have no resistance to offer and you will do better than you've ever done because you can't offer a fight. The real <u>you</u> is now."

I looked around. Charles looked startled and Dave frightened, but chastened, but he did go on and he performed better than I've ever seen him do before. It was strange, because I had no conscious awareness of speaking and it didn't feel like it was me who had uttered these words.

In October 2006, I took my black belt test. It was harder than my service in the army had ever been, but at the end of it I realised that I was no longer the angry and frightening man who had started aikido. I had found a new sort of humanity.

I'm still the soldier that began this story, but I have been given the chance to truly live. Aikido, you sorted out my life. You gave me compassion and I am afraid of no one. I am not stuck in my painful past. Now I have hope. I can talk to people instead of wanting to dislocate their spine from their neck. My desire now is to heal. Aikido, from my heart, "Thank you!"

気 気 気

The Heart of the Matter
by
Paul Rest - Sofia University Dojo - U.S.A. - 3rd Dan

I look at my life as being split in two; before I started aikido and afterwards. I say this because aikido totally transformed my life and my art. (I am a professional artist).

It was a slow process because although I considered myself athletic as I swam, ran, lifted weights, played racquetball and handball, when I stepped on the mat, I was all left feet. It took me many years to untangle myself and my energy, and to begin to feel a sense of flow with what was happening on the mat and off it.

To backup a little, I have always had 'the creative urge,' as my parents would apologetically explain to the neighbors after I drew on their sidewalks with colored chalk. But as I grew up, getting that out of me and into actual form was a laborious process that took years. Aikido brought about this transformation as it gave me the confidence to trust the creative voice inside me.

Perhaps the biggest discovery I made was to eventually understand that creativity is not just an idea, it is a somatic process and as such, it impacts on our bodies. It is a process that has to involve all of me, every fiber and cell. This realization altered my life and only then could I access that deep unending well of creativity within myself.

There was one incident in particular that sticks in my mind. I had just put together the sale of a very special painting by the famed Renaissance artist, Sandro Botticelli. It was a portrait of the famous Simonetta (his model for "Birth of Venus" and many other paintings). The sale came together with a lot of hard work and more than a little luck.

The painting had been viewed and approved by the buyer's representative. The one remaining step was the wire transfer of funds. But just as this was about to happen, there was an economic downturn in the buyer's home country (Japan) and the sale fell through at the very last moment.

I remember thinking that I had put all this energy into selling someone else's painting rather than something I had created. Somehow, I felt the disappointment would be easier to take if it had been my own work. There was a growing feeling inside me that that I was focusing my energy in the wrong place and that I was failing to be true to myself.

It felt much the same on the mat. I was out of balance. I would move my right foot rather than my left. My arms and hands became mixed up. I would turn the wrong way or forget to turn at all. Once during a class I forgot how to do a two-step, one of the most basic movements in aikido. Another time I realized that every time I turned, I was closing my eyes for a few seconds. My breathing was off and out of sync with my body movements. My heart wasn't yet open on the mat.

I would hear my teachers say over and over again, "Find your center." So this became a mantra for me on and off the mat. I would ask myself whenever I remembered it, whether I was driving or maybe taking a shower, "Where's your center, Paul?"

I had read books about the *hara* and during *zazen* meditation I would go there, to my center. But aikido involved movements, and lots of them and I couldn't find the place I knew from sitting *zazen* when moving on the mat.

Nonetheless as I continued to ask this question, I noticed that certain aspects of my life were changing. At first these changes were small, almost imperceptible. There were moments when time seemed to slow down both on and off the mat. I began to notice things on a deeper level. I would see colors and motion, but these moments would only last for a second or two and only every now and then. Previously, I had always been able to assess colors and color combinations within a painting quickly. I knew immediately whether any particular painting felt right and whether it would sell. I was usually right! This would all happen in a moment. It was calculating or to be more blunt, without heart.

But something else was changing now, although I did not realise it at first. I was looking at artwork from a different perspective and would take in more detail. I was doing the same on the mat too. Arms and feet that had seemed a blur to me when an instructor was demonstrating a technique were now registering.

I would later realize that this was because I was more centered. It was a slow and gradual process, but even a glacial shift is a shift. When observing art, I could see variations in colors and patterns that were new to me. On the mat, I began to move my center more and much to my surprise and astonishment, my arms and legs seemed to follow. Not in perfect harmony yet, but things were showing up, which brought me no end of delight. I noticed my training partners were beginning to move with me and respond in ways I had only dreamed about before.

As I took my *kyu* tests, this process continued. Meantime, there was a financial recession in America and my art business collapsed. However, I realized that although the outer form of my business was gone, I still had good connections with many collectors, and of course, I still knew a lot about art and how to find good art, so I survived on a much-scaled down basis.

This gave me the space to become an artist in my own right. I worked on a novel and wrote articles and painted watercolors and oils. I gave one to one of my *sensei*, who much to my surprise, hung it in the *dojo*. I entered another oil in a juried show and again to my surprise, it was accepted. A short time later, a serious art collector visited my studio and wished to buy an unfinished oil that was leaning against the wall. I was stunned. All the while I kept asking that question,

"Where is your center, Paul? Listen to it. Talk to it."

As I became more skilled on the mat, my art shifted even more. By the time I took my 2nd *kyu* test, I was beginning to have a glimpse of what I could be. It was still a bit murky, but it was there nevertheless. I began to appreciate that by developing my artistic talents, I could make a living out of art, music, writing and perhaps more. By way of evidence, the first article I submitted for publication years before had been accepted. Later, a Sunday news magazine, for a big city newspaper, accepted one of my essays and this was happening more regularly. I also noticed that when I wrote from my center, and my heart, these pieces tended to find a receptive ear with editors. I wondered if, perhaps, this could happen with my painting too, and with everything else in my life.

By the time I was ready to take my *shodan* test, the quest, of living life from my center, seemed huge. In retrospect, as I developed, more was expected of me from those around me. Sometimes there are moments on the mat, when you are forced to dig deep to find what is needed to go on and this is what I now had to do off the mat. The problem I had to solve was how to bridge the gap between having a creative idea, and making it a reality. I would often write the ideas down but they would stay there on the page. It was like watching a spark trying to jump from one pole to another and not making it.

I still managed to sell a painting here and there and get a few essays and book reviews published and it was enough to keep me in business, but this was a grim time and somehow to move on, I had to dig deep within myself.

I began to write about aikido, and the articles were accepted and published by editors. Things *were* happening! I wrote a short story and showed it to a number of friends. One said,

"You've found your voice."

And so I had. Another short story followed and another. These were all published in a well-known literary journal in South America).

On the mat, things began to shift too. My first big realization was that my center was never static. It was alive, always moving, changing, growing, reaching out and it was always there and available to me. It was a really important discovery. Second, I realized that working with my center needed some effort and work on my part. Sometimes I just had to be quiet and listen and other times I had to consciously reach down into that well of power, creativity and inspiration. I had to be the person that both acted and listened. I couldn't just be the audience waiting to be entertained. Third, I realized that there is a mystery here that is unfathomable. Whatever the center, my center, everyone's center is or isn't, most of it is beyond words or understanding.

Finally I understood that there will always be an ebb and flow with my creativity both on, the mat and off it. I was told a number of the times to think of my training as like a desert. There would be some highs and lows, but more often than not there would be a long journey through what seemed to be dry, barren country. The same was true for my creativity. But as those of you who have visited deserts know, what might seems to be a barren landscape at first glance is in fact filled with life and beauty.

Now I understood the importance of practice. It was important to keep writing and painting, even if it didn't appear to me that I was totally on the mark, just as it was to keep training on the mat. With both, it was okay to make mistakes, because that is how we learn.

All my creative ideas don't always find a home and come into reality and often my aikido isn't what I want it to be either. However, if I'm there, present, working from my center, I can laugh and learn from what doesn't work and celebrate the mystery of creation with what does work.

I keep reminding myself that at the heart of the mystery, is heart.

気　気　気

Searching for the Light
by
Neil Rowlingson - Burwell Aikido Club - England - 5th Kyu

As a sufferer of depression on and off throughout my adult life, I have made many changes to my lifestyle to try and alleviate the symptoms. I have a more balanced diet and I drink less alcohol. In the past, I never used to do much exercise, but I started karate two years ago and I've even started running recently. I also practise cognitive behavioural therapy (CBT).

I'm physically healthier, but more importantly, all of these things have helped to shorten my episodes of depression and make them easier to cope with.

Eighteen months ago I started aikido, and this has not only had a very positive impact on the depression itself, but also seems to enhance the impact of some of the other activities that I have just mentioned.

The first basic benefit is that it keeps me active and adds to my fitness. It may not be as strenuous a work-out as karate or a run, but it's certainly more relaxing and a whole lot better than vegetating in front of the telly. Feeling fitter not only makes me feel better because of the physical impact, but also because it's given me a sense of pride and achievement. I have never felt so good in all my life, and it's all down to my own efforts. What is more, the fitter I become, the better it gets and the easier it becomes.

Secondly, I take pride in learning a difficult and very interesting skill. Setting goals and achieving them has given me a big psychological boost, especially as I have to work so hard to attain them. In aikido, I feel that my progress has been slow but that's more due to my intermittent attendance due to injuries (not as a result of my aikido practice) and other commitments. Nonetheless, even I can see that I'm making progress, and that makes me feel good.

Probably the thing that I like the most about aikido is that it's simply fun. Although there is a certain level of discipline required to ensure that the practice is safe for all, the class is very relaxed and there is a lot of laughter. *Sensei* injects a lot of humour into the lessons and the members of our club are very friendly, so it's easy to spend time with them. The whole lesson takes on a social aspect that a dedicated exercise class or a more formal martial arts lesson can lack. Regardless of any other benefit aikido brings, I usually leave with a big smile on my face, which helps with depression significantly.

On a more subtle level, aikido has helped me become more aware of myself and my surroundings. It reinforces and enhances my work with CBT, as part of that requires me to practice mindfulness. I am encouraged to live in the moment rather than worrying about the future or the past. Aikido requires me to do the same; to be aware of my body and how grounded I feel, as well as learning to move from my centre. I have to do all that whilst staying connected to my partner. I need to be aware of their movement and intent and learn how to blend with this. Everything else has to be left behind and it is the same when practising mindfulness within CBT. I just have to be aware or my surroundings and my body and live that moment, rather than letting anything else distract me.

Whether you're eating and trying to focus on the individual tastes and textures of each mouthful, or walking the dog and concentrating on the sights and sounds around you, or any other activity, mindfulness helps you experience the present. This has helped reduce the negative thought and anxiety that are typically associated with depression. In short, when I am able to do this, I feel more alive and appreciate the present more fully, rather than worrying about what may happen in the future. Aikido reinforces my CBT work and vice versa.

There are other aspects of aikido which also help me deal with depression, but perhaps all I need to say is that I simply enjoy it, and I love the idea that many years from now, I will be able to do what some of the senior grades do. It is a beautiful art when done well and anyone watching it is almost certainly left with a desire to be able to do the same.

I live in hope!

気 気 気

Walking the Plank
by
Matt Townsend - Cambridge Aiki Dojo - England - 1st Kyu

Back in my home town in darkest Essex I was heading to my college. This was my sixth year of making the same journey. However, this day would be very different from most. The housing estate I lived on had a river and dual carriageway that ran parallel to it, and to get to the other side, you had to cross one bridge and go through an underpass. At this time in the morning, the route was always busy as a procession of boys in their navy blue uniforms trudged disconsolately on their way to school.

As I crossed the bridge, I saw three year-seven boys, the youngest year in the school. They would have been 11 or 12 years of age. As I approached, I heard them using language unbefitting of their age.

As a sixth former, a former prefect and their senior, I thought I'd make light of the situation and as I passed them I said, "Ah bless. You're the smallest gangsters I've ever seen," and patted one of them on the head.

This was a mistake. Their surprise turned to disdain and they started to follow me, shouting abuse and threats. I was willing to tolerate and ignore this, as after all, I may have spoken out of turn, but then, one of them grabbed a short plank of wood, a fence panel discarded in the underpass, and I noticed that it still had nails sticking out of it.

Now I had a problem! If I kept walking, I might be hurt or perhaps look like a fool to my friends. Likewise I didn't want to fight and hurt these three much younger children, as that too would look bad and felt wrong.

I think the option I chose flowed from my aikido training. At that time, I had a few years of practice and had attained fourth *kyu*. I turned and faced them on the far side of the underpass. All three were now in front of me. I could see that the boy with the plank of wood was standing, as if he were playing baseball, ready to swing. It felt and looked as if he were preparing for a *yokomenuchi* strike. Knowing this, I stepped forward and entered deeply, shouting, *(kiai)*, point blank into his face. He fell backwards. I stepped over him to collect the plank of wood and threw it into a bush. The other two stood in shock for a second, and then the smaller one tried to kick me in the leg. I maintained a strong posture and I let him connect. It became evident that he was more used to kicking footballs than people and he recoiled in pain.

As I walked away, the first boy was still on his back, being comforted by the other two. A pang of guilt hit me. I could argue that I didn't touch him, which was true, but this wasn't a brave or noble deed by any measure, and so I kept it quiet. I later consoled myself knowing that no one was seriously hurt, the children had learnt their lesson, and I didn't lose face or any teeth.

A few years later, during my undergraduate degree, I went back to the school to help teach. I found out that the child with the plank of wood had come from a broken home. His father was a local drug dealer who was in and out of prison. The child had ultimately been expelled from the school because of 'behavioural issues'. It was clear that he had not had the best start in life. So whilst it seems that the way I handled the situation did not significantly change the path that he was travelling, I would like to think that at least I did not add to his woes. I do now feel that I dealt with the situation in as positive a way as was possible.

It was a good example of how aikido could be used to resolve a situation with the minimum of fuss and has provided me with motivation ever since to continue my training.

Create Each Day Anew
by
Paul King - Institute of Aikido Auckland - New Zealand - 6th Kyu

"One day at a time."

I've just achieved my first sober year. I have a key chain full of sober tags, t-shirts from my rehab hospital celebrating various milestones and a sterling silver pendant of the number one, made by my wonderful wife. At some point I will pass on this pendant to someone that feels right and has also achieved their 'one year'. A friend did something similar for me, when she gave me a framed serenity prayer that had been given to her six years previously.

During this process of recovery, which to a great extent was because of aikido, the following words have inspired me.

"Nothing great was ever achieved without overcoming great obstacles, and no hero of history deserves more acclaim than those who were triumphant over self."

If you do recognise these words, then we have more in common than aikido. They were not uttered by O Sensei, nor any other *sensei*, though you would be forgiven for thinking so. In fact, they are contained in an AA publication by Hazelden and are the last written words I had from the late and great Tom Claunch. He saved my life by getting me into Capri, my rehab hospital, of which he was the co-founder.

I entered the place on a stretcher. It was discovered later than I had internal bleeding from a stomach ulcer. I didn't get out of the wheelchair for the first six days without assistance. I'd done some damage.

When I told *Sensei* about it, he didn't blink. He just told me he was proud of me for getting sober and that now the real work starts. It would start with getting my ass back into the *dojo* and he said,

"Do whatever you can, but do come" (I've heard those words so many times since).

The important word was CAN'. It still is. It's the same discipline I learned in rehab from my wonderful case manager Brent Smith. 'DO what you CAN, but DO,' 'Progress not perfection' and many other memorable live-by phrases.

The lessons I learnt in rehab were consistent with what I was being taught on the mat. Initially, I had simply turned up, even though I didn't really understood what was going on. My *sensei*, Dunken Francis, made me concentrate on weapons work. This was because I was so weak and in so much pain that I couldn't do the pins, throws or *ukemi* that I needed to learn for my first grading. I was given a 70% chance of being able to walk again and virtually no chance being able to walk properly. Weapons were a way of keeping the discipline of showing up and gave me a chance to begin the process of change without the risk of serious injury.

But practising aikido, even in this fairly limited way, literally re-booted my brain and got me back on the road. So whilst I have passed no grading, (whereas I have all manner of awards for my solid recovery from alcohol), aikido and all that came with it, my *sensei* and the people I've associated with as a result of my practise, were central to my recovery. I can also say with certainty that without it, things would be very different for me now.
Sensei describes my progress in aikido as "epic." It has been slow and very painful. The physical damage meant that I was in constant pain until relatively recently, but I just kept coming back. That's not it though. The cognitive behavioural therapy and mindful thinking practices I've learned in rehab and recovery are *exactly* the same as those used in aikido. Being in the moment, using mindful thinking – the Zen inspired psychotherapy technique I use all the time, is sharply focused by the sitting in *seiza*, breathing correctly, focusing on O Sensei, participating in the bowing in and the claps which begin and end training. The principle that on the mat is aikido and nothing but aikido is so immensely powerful and healing. Keeping my *gi*, my nails and my body clean out of respect for my fellow practitioners, and vitally, our responsibility to look after our partner, all play their part.

Sensei couldn't get to my one-year celebration. He pointedly said he'd come to my twentieth. (He's always telling me in a 'Marvin, the paranoid android' way that the first two decades in aikido are the worst, after that it gets really hard). I'm an *aiki*-baby and have had to be treated as such. I had to learn to roll from all fours, roll around on my back to find balance points, even wear gloves in training (my hands have been susceptible to cuts). I've had to practice my first *bokken* cut over and over again. I have had to practice the 31 *jo kata* on my own for entire classes.

The point is PROGRESS, NOT PERFECTION. Recovery from alcohol dependency creates a super A+ 'you' because of the self-examination and correction in attitudes, habits and thinking you have to go through. However, you can never achieve perfection. Aikido is the same; the reasons are obvious.

As *Sensei* explained to us a while back, our responsibility is to simply show up and to do what we can, while we develop an understanding of why we individually practice aikido.

Even if you have an 'owie,'

"There's always a way to train around injury, come and do what you can." he said.

His job was to understand what those reasons were and thereby guide us. As you've read, I'm new, so I can't really say too much more about my experience of aikido in a technical sense. I can, however, recommend that if you, or anyone you know is in a situation similar to mine, then practising aikido should be seriously considered.

It would be wrong not to add that my recovery and to be honest, improvement, (massive improvement), was not solely down to aikido. Tom Claunch, who I mentioned earlier, saved my life by giving my wonderful wife the courage to hand me over to his care for detox and rehab. She, along with some of my family and my friends also played a huge part.

However, aikido was a central part of the process and I emphasise this when I tell my story in the work I now do as a speaker and coach.

Three people much cleverer and wiser than I told me three things;

Tom Claunch told me,

"You can't have a drink, even if you think your ass is falling off."

Brent Smith (my case manager and continuing mentor in recovery) told me,

"You're just having a bad day, everyone has them. Don't drink and your head won't fall off."

Sensei Dunken Francis (along with many other less printable things) told me,

"Come to training and DO what you CAN."

Now it's my turn to give back some of what I have been given. I'll be bringing a new person to training with me this week, someone also in recovery. I hope he gets it, too. Also, I have been asked to personally sponsor (mentor) someone only a few weeks into recovery. A huge honour and responsibility and given how it came about, a great vote of confidence in the solidity of my recovery.

I wonder if I can get him into a *dojo*, too.

Editor's note - *Since writing this piece Paul took his 6th kyu exam,(a requirement in his particular aikido school), and 13 months after being in a wheelchair, he passed.*

気 気 気

Seeing the Spirals
by
Jamie Leno Zimron - 5th Dan - U.S.A.

The treasure chest of early black-and-white aikido footage contains an array of instructional classics, including O Sensei and Koichi Tohei, working with golfers and baseball players. Films like these serve as direct examples of the founder himself taking training off the mat, into daily life and worldly professions. The connection with golf, it turns out, is also wonderfully direct. During the same period that the Samurai played such a leading part in Japanese life, Scottish warriors referred to their swords as irons. Harkening back to centuries ago in the land where golf was born, golfers today wield irons and in modern golf jargon affectionately call their clubs their 'blades' and 'sticks.' And they worry most about 'slicing', 'cutting across' and 'killing' the ball.

I began training in aikido when I was 21, and have been golfing since age seven. My parents started playing, so I did too. It seemed I had a natural ability to swing smoothly and get around a golf course in relatively few strokes. I won the Wisconsin state championships and gained national ranking in the Junior Girls Top Ten. But instead of playing college golf, I dove into aikido, because Title IX legislation had not yet kicked in to provide athletic scholarships for young women in America.

It turned out these were the early heydays of the 'Art of Peace' taking root in the San Francisco Bay Area, where I now lived. So it was full-on aikido for me, with only occasional forays onto the golf course when I visited my folks.

During those first years on the mat, I always had a feeling all throughout my body, like on-the-tip-of-my-tongue, that 'I know this.' Yet, I could never quite identify what was so familiar. Then one day at my *dojo* while teaching how to hold a *bokken* (wooden sword) these words spilled out: "It's a lot like holding a golf club!"

Suddenly, I got it, what that feeling was, and the connections seemed so obvious. *Kokyunage* throws to the rear and forward reminded me of a backswing and downswing. Golfers' hands actually do a *kokyu* 'wrist cock' at the top of the backswing and follow-through, and apply *yonkyo* on the club handle as the club head is hitting the ball to create powerful impact. Extending energy to the tip of the sword or face of the club, getting grounded in a stable stance, spiraling center and hips, maintaining alignment and connection, focusing the mind as sharply as a samurai. It was all there, and this was just for starters.

In 1996, I was suffering from a bit of a mid-life crisis, having left my *dojo* and bodywork/therapy practice in San Francisco, moved off to a foreign land, and returned not knowing what was next in my work or life. I was feeling the effects of too many injuries (yes, mostly from aikido), plus adrenal exhaustion, and knew I needed to take some time out to heal.

I re-settled in sunny San Diego and was feeling better when Dena, my best friend since kindergarten in Milwaukee, came to visit. She had taken up golf and asked me for a lesson. So off we went to the driving range at Torrey Pines. She brought a 7-iron and 3-wood, I brought my bokken.

The way to grip a golf club and a samurai sword really is virtually the same, except that in golf, the hands touch and two fingers overlap. The sword showed clearly how the clubface needs to be 'square' when impacting the golf ball, otherwise people slice or cut-across the shot. We adjusted Dena's posture and stance so she felt centered and grounded when addressing the ball. She worked on remaining stable and in balance, while shifting her weight laterally through the swing. Rather than trying to kill the ball or hit with brute muscle force, we considered using *ki*. We talked about relaxed rhythm and breath-power, with body and mind working in synchronized sequential motion (*Ai*).

Soon, Dena started engaging the power in her core and lower body, and making *kata*-like swings with proper positions, transitions and sequenced movement. Instead of making erratic attempts to hit the ball with her hands or arms, she was making more technically sound, repeatable golf swings. In barely an hour, almost like magic, she started hitting all these beautiful soaring golf shots – and with consistency, over and over again. Then suddenly, ecstatically, she fell on the ground, threw her feet and club in the air, and shouted out,

"This is like enlightenment! You've got to teach this stuff to the world!"

For me, this was one of those life-changing moments. There was an aura around that whole hour, and I felt as if I were being guided by some greater force and source. While Dena was in the grass exclaiming, I suddenly felt connected to a part of me that for too long I had ignored and hadn't appreciated. It was as though an innate intelligence moved through me like a giant aikido spiral, sweeping past elements of my being into the present and revealing shape and flow into the future. Without knowing it then, the seeds were planted for what would soon grow into KiAi Golf and The KiAi Way, the next vehicles for extending my *aiki*-based work in the world.

A Way to Reconcile the World

How amazing to see this universal energy flow, transcending our own mind and self, working through our lives. Aikido continues to help me understand and find words for what I seemed to naturally know as a seven-year old, just swinging away and chasing golf balls down the fairway. The golf course has turned into an outdoor *dojo* in the expanses of grass and sky. I'm so grateful for both aikido and golf, and actually blown away every day, not only by all the chances to train, but by the revealing of these magnificent convergences and forward spirallings along life's journey.

We never really do know the what, or where, or when, or how,... but 'it' seems to, all on its great *aiki* own!

> "Move like a beam of light.
> Spiral in circles
> Around a stable center."
> *O'Sensei haiku*

Golf is "an odyssey, an adventure from hole to hole ...
world upon world,
a vehicle for training our higher capacities,
the ultimate discipline for transcendence...
the alignment of human consciousness
with the physical forces of the universe ...
The grace that comes from such a discipline,
the extra feel in the hands, the extra strength and knowin',
all those special powers ye've felt from time to time,
begin to enter our lives."

Shivas Irons, Fictitious Golf Mystic in Michael Murphy's 'Golf In The Kingdom,'
1971

気　気　気

Travelling
by
Rebekah Tait - Aikido Yuishinkai Aberdeen - Scotland - 4th Kyu

The road I've journeyed on has not been a long one, and there is still such a long way to go, but to measure it by duration might be hasty. In my experience, short though it may be, Aristotle's assertion generally holds true;

"The whole is more than the sum of its parts."

To illustrate this, I can detail my aikido journey thus far:

9th May 2011 – The film 'Hanna' is released (an inspirational female character with kickass skills) that made me look into martial arts as a real practice rather than just an idea.

16th May 2011 – I turn up (shaking the whole way there) to my local Yuishinkai Aikido *dojo*.

19th May 2011 – I'm hooked to a twice-weekly fix of aikido with a group of outstanding people.

9th July 2011 – My first seminar away from home.

13th Aug 2011 – My first grading.

10th Sept 2011 – My first seminar experience of aikido out with Yuishinkai.

Fast-forward through the next few months of practice, various seminars and extra morning practice (interjected with the odd flirtation with tai chi and Pilates) on to...

May 2012 – One year on I attend a seminar with the man himself *Sensei* Koretoshi Maruyama.

On a few more months, seminars, bumps and bruises and that's where I am today.

Other than a shade or two more colour on my belt, and a few boxes ticked on my '*sensei's* to learn from before you die' list, the parts don't mean that much without a bit of context. My life as a whole, there has been one filled with adventure and there have been a few dragons to slay. So let me paint the picture.

I thought I knew how to live my life and I was accustomed to following my dreams until I was faced with the death of a loved one back home, when I was thousands of miles away in Taiwan. It made me realise that I wasn't really living at all. I felt alone and vulnerable which was terrifying. I began to realise that I didn't know who I was.

To clarify, the concept of going away to 'find one's self' always seemed to me contrived and self-indulgent. You are who you live out. Going somewhere else can give you the social space to re-think things, but in my opinion, if you don't deal with things in-situ, then it's very easy to become someone for whom the grass is always greener on the other side.

As I stood on the rooftop of my dormitory in Taiwan, I realised that I had been one of those people. Four years prior, I had got stuck in a malicious, abusive relationship and I could see that since I ended this, whilst I had left with exploration in mind, all I had been doing was running away. Now, it felt like I had lost my way. I could see that I was living a life of contradiction, exploring my Christian faith, whilst dabbling with the seedier side of life by dabbling in Tai Pei's underworld, doing stupid things like taking drunken moped rides and getting involved in mild scuffs with the Yakuza to prove I wasn't scared, when in fact I was terrified.

All of this brought me home to Scotland to finish university and grieve. I was to find that instead of coming back to the security I anticipated, my world would be turned upside down, because I was to learn something about my family that I had never known.

The person, who had died wasn't as biologically close to me, as I'd been lead to believe for 21 years. I was left numb and feeling like an empty shell. I felt betrayed. I literally had no idea who I was. Again I could not face it and I kept it as my secret for a year, focusing on keeping things together on the outside, whilst falling apart within. So much so, that by the time I graduated, I was using alcohol to sleep and caffeine to wake. I couldn't go on.

On the outside, no one could see this. I won awards, held exhibitions in galleries I couldn't have dreamt of. Yet I didn't feel any of it, and the final straw came when I lost my best friend.

I was forced to take stock of my life and look for ways in which I could develop mind, body and soul. I had been helping out a humanitarian organisation on and off for some years and I knew they were offering a creative internship in New York, which seemed ideal; so I took it.

It was. I was living with what felt like my second family and being loved to death (in a very non British way), while being given the opportunity to get to know loads of homeless and struggling people, to whom I could give some love.

I found some peace, but when I returned to the UK, it wasn't long before I was mixing with some of the people I'd been avoiding, and the addictions I had previously overcome, began to rear their ugly heads once more. Eating disorders and (to a lesser extent) alcohol were how I dealt with things, and once more I lost my way.

My body was a stranger. I loathed it. It changed shape. It craved what damaged it. It wasn't mine.

So once more I looked to escape. I took up an invitation to join a small team of folks working alongside a couple of orphanages and schools in Kenya. I had an amazing time. Playing and being creative with hundreds of kids on the mainland and Lamu Island would inspire the hardest of hearts. It fed my soul and blew my mind, but despite this, I could not escape my demons and I began to hate my body even more and the result was that I started to disassociate myself from those around me.

How could someone who claimed to 'love' other people and care for them mind, body and soul do this? It felt so wrong that here were these children with virtually nothing and here was I, with so much to be thankful for, cursing and abusing everything I'd been given.

When I reached a doll-sized frame, something finally snapped and I began to get help. My self-esteem was at rock bottom, but I slowly began to realise that I was not broken, I was simply in need of some repair.

A Way to Reconcile the World

After a few years, there was a massive change in how I viewed the world and I thought I had it sorted. Slowly I had opened up to my family and friends and through many tearful painful conversations, I found love and respect for them. They gave me (and still do) unconditional love.

However, one spring, on an arty trip to Barcelona with a friend, I had a very frightening experience, resulting from a very close shave with a dangerous man on a train in the countryside. It left me with a horrid feeling of vulnerability. I felt anger and shame at my perceived weakness, which made me feel sick.

And so we come to 'Hanna' and the start of my aikido journey.

It was such a gift. For the first time in my life I began to see myself as a person. Not just 'Rebekah' – the artist/mind/soul searcher. I had fingers! And toes! And they wanted to play!

To those who've never been there, this probably seems silly, but I hadn't realised how disconnected I had become from my body. It was a thing that got me around, that didn't like the limits I pushed it to, but practicing aikido gave me the space to breathe,…with lungs! I became aware of my centre, because it was essential to the fun, not because I wanted to criticise or abuse it.

The freedom I felt (and still feel) was indescribable. It opened doors to so much more. I gained the courage in body, and literal physical stability, to do a trek to a remote village in the Himalayas. Watching locals skip over the mountains with the most amazing grace and control and (slightly bossily) sharing aikido techniques with my fellow trekkers, to take care of our muscles at the close of day. For the first time in my life I felt what it was like for my mind to be quiet, my soul to sing and my body to be alive, all at the same time. Half way up some mountain climb, feet dangling over the cliff edge, I began to paint for the first time in years.

Over the years following university, I had disconnected somewhat from art. I'd developed a slightly voyeuristic view of the world, as though watching other people live it. Creating art had become too painful to bear, tapping into parts of me I couldn't control.

But not now. I slowly began to get a studio together and after being in Nepal, I began watching the world around me reveal some of its mysteries, seen through 'owned' eyes. Passion that had begun to re-emerge was given a massive kick forward by aikido as it re-engaged my love of exploration, but this time I wanted to touch the world around me and as such, a rather large amount of seriously large paintings were born.

I'm not perfect, far from it, and aikido hasn't created a super woman with no vulnerabilities or weaknesses, but it's given me the space to begin to understand my physical limitations, my uniqueness, and to own them, as something to work with, instead of fear.

I had been working on getting my life together for a while, but aikido has played a crucial part in getting my act together, as it has opened a door and given me a perspective of life that I never thought I'd get and it accessed a part of me that I didn't know existed.

Life and living are now something to be played with and enjoyed, (when really lucky, through the eyes of a three year old). For that, and the amazing people I practice with, I am very grateful. I love them all very much and never fail to be amazed at how many other lovely people there are out there journeying with aikido too. Their stories may be different but the basic motivation seems the same, aikido not only as a physical tool, but as part of daily life.

気　気　気

When You Have Spiritual Protection, You Don't Need Martial Protection
by
Miles Kessler - Integral Dojo Tel Aviv - Israel - 5th Dan

It was early 1998. I had just finished an eight-year phase of life, living in Japan. I had studied aikido full time with Morihiro Saito Sensei, at the famous Iwama *dojo*. There was a sense of deep satisfaction in what I had accomplished, and yet there was also a subtle itch of wanting something more, something I wasn't finding in my life in Japan.

When I left Japan at the end of 1997 I was told by Saito Sensei to return to the U.S. and start teaching aikido. In many ways I was ready for this commitment. I had been training intensively in Iwama for eight years, was in my mid-thirties, had gotten my 4th *dan*, had become fluent in Japanese, and was translating for Sensei. I had learned much about Japanese culture from the inside, and I had been teaching aikido two times a week in Japan for three years. I felt I had achieved much and the confidence in who I had become served as a solid foundation upon which I had built my identity. However, beneath all my confidence I could not deny that there was something missing. I had a spiritual calling that could no longer be denied and it was this that was to guide my next move.

It seemed that all of my growth and development, as valuable and beautiful as it was, was only touching one dimension of my existence, spreading out nicely on the surface, but not penetrating to the core of my being. So I decided to travel for a year to seek out spiritual teachers and undertake formal spiritual practices.

During the last three years in Japan I had taken on regular self practices which included "A Course in Miracles", and daily 30 minute meditations. These were all informal self practices done without a teacher, or guide that were largely inspired by the many spiritual books that I was reading at the time. Two of the books that had a particular impact on me, were by American Vipassana teachers; Joseph Goldstein and Jack Kornfeld. Both of them had practiced in Burma and from all the teachers they spoke about in their books, one name kept catching my attention. A teacher named U Pandita, (which karmically worked its way deep into my consciousness). I really connected with the method of practice that they taught, and with that inspiration I decided to make my way to Burma to practice Vipassana meditation.

Even though I was sure I wanted to commit to a formal spiritual practice, I was still quite attached to my own ideas (and baggage) about aikido being a 'spiritual path'. After all, O Sensei's life was a testament to the classic spiritual journey. So when I began my own spiritual journey, I managed to pack the 'Spiritual Aikido' ideal tightly into my traveller's backpack. I did this by conveniently planning that my visit to Burma would coincide with an aikido seminar that a Japanese teacher friend of mine would be leading. My plan was to do a 10-day retreat, then the one-week aikido seminar, followed by another 10-day retreat. Spiritual practice and aikido practice. I had arranged things nicely so I could have my cake and eat it too. Perfect....or so I thought!

After a two-month teaching stint in New Zealand, and some rest and relaxation in Thailand, I decided it was time to get on track with the main purpose of my trip, meditation in Burma. I caught a plane to Rangoon and made a bee-line to the Panditarama Meditation Center, and to U Pandita himself.

Upon arriving at the center, I was told that Sayadaw U Pandita was away for the day and wouldn't get back until the evening. I was told to check into a hotel and come back the next day. I explained that I had come a long way, and that I was there to meditate, so they allowed me to sit and wait in the office until U Pandita got back. He eventually did return after seven hours, and when he was told I had been waiting to see him, he glanced over his shoulder at me (I had a sense that he was sizing me up), and he agreed, with a slight sense of irritation, to interview me. I was quite confident I could overcome what seemed to be U Pandita's first impression of me. Having learned much about discipline and proper etiquette while living in Japan, I did my best to showcase these qualities to him. In fact, I was sure U Pandita would be impressed. After all, who wouldn't be?

When I entered U Pandita's quarters, I was immediately struck by his strong presence. It completely dominated the room, indeed the whole meditation center. I also had an uneasy sense that he saw a part of me that

I wasn't seeing. So whilst there was an immediate feeling of trust, I also felt exposed and unsettled in a very subtle way. Nonetheless, I did my best to make a favorable impression while answering through the translator several questions from U Pandita.

He asked about my background in meditation (self practice for the past two years), my purpose for coming to meditation, (spiritual liberation), and why Panditarama, (I wanted to train in the Mahasi tradition). U Pandita also asked me about my plans in Burma and I made a feeble attempt to explain that I planned to do a 10-day retreat, then leave to attend the aikido seminar for a week, after which I'd come back for another ten days of meditation practice. He briefly asked what aikido was, but it seemed that this got lost in translation, and I didn't think he got it. Nonetheless, it didn't feel like the right time for further explanation, but I was sure that if the opportunity ever arose again to have a conversation about aikido and spirituality, then all would be well. For now all that mattered was that U Pandita agreed to allow me to stay and practice on probation. I was in!

During the next ten days of practice, I received daily interviews and Dharma talks with U Pandita and I soon understood why he had such a renowned reputation. Here was the master I had been seeking my whole life. Having been a monk for more than 70 years and a meditation teacher for 50, his wisdom and skillful guidance was like nothing I had ever encountered before. But even more impressive was his presence as a spiritual warrior. I had never experienced in another person such complete fearlessness, confidence, uncompromising determination and skill in teaching. I didn't really have the capacity to understand it fully, but U Pandita had a strength that was unshakable. It would take me many, many months of practicing on retreat, indeed a few years, before I began to understand the source of that unshakable strength. Here was a man deeply grounded in the absolute truth, the 'Dhamma' of ultimate reality, and it literally made everything in me that was relative, feel extremely limited. I knew that here, in this teacher, I could place my absolute trust.

The irony did not escape me. I had spent much of my life in the martial arts seeking for the warrior ideal. Now here I was meeting that ideal in the form of a simple monk. A man who was deftly wielding the sword of truth, the shield of concentration, and all with a heart of loving kindness and compassion.

A Way to Reconcile the World

U Pandita taught that 100% of all the suffering in the world had its source in the mind. The world, he said, is full of external enemies, but it is the internal enemies that are far more dangerous. These enemies come in the form of mental impurities and the purification of the mind is where all true battles must be fought. In this, he was uncompromising and relentless. He would be brutally direct when necessary. The Buddha, he taught, was like a doctor who knew exactly which medicine was needed to cure or awaken the patient. All the medicines he gave fell into two types; sweet medicine (loving kindness, compassion and support), and bitter medicine (truth, discipline and challenge). U Pandita, as he often unapologetically claimed, gave the bitter medicine. Sooner or later, all yogis got to experience a full dose of his tough love. And then if they managed to stick around, they also had the experience of its cure. I had finally found the teacher I wanted to be practicing with, the practice I wanted to be doing, and the place I wanted to be practicing. This was it! I just had to go and attend an aikido seminar and then I'd be right back.

So when the first ten days were finished, I packed my backpack and headed off to the seminar. On my way out I stopped in the center's office to let them know that I would be back in one week. The office staff member stepped out to pass on my news and upon returning I was told, much to my surprise, that in fact, I could not come back. Of course there must have been some misunderstanding. I insisted on meeting with U Pandita to explain my situation and get permission to return. I was confident I could clear this up.

I was asked once again to wait, and so I sat in U Pandita's interview room meditating, and working out the story I would tell him, so that I could come back. After about three hours, I was finally taken to see U Pandita, as he was overseeing the unloading of a new Buddha statue to the monastery. In another moment of irony, I thought to myself, "The Buddha has just arrived, and I am leaving". So there we all were, on some sort of cosmic-karmic threshold. the incoming Buddha, U Pandita, and the outgoing me.

U Pandita gave me half of his attention and asked what I wanted. I explained my situation with the aikido seminar and that I would be back in a week for more practice. He told me that I had done well, but I couldn't come back until the next time I was in Burma. I agreed that I hadn't planned things well, but explained that I had to go to the aikido event. I apologized for this and said I was sorry that I was leaving in the middle of my stay, and told him that I really wanted to come back and continue the practice in a week. Yet, somehow, U Pandita didn't seem moved by my display of sincerity.

I was beginning to feel that my reasons for leaving were perhaps a little weak, but I was convinced that this was a legitimate excuse. If I could just convey that to U Pandita, surely he would understand. After all, we were talking about aikido, a spiritual martial art, and it was just a matter of convincing him. So I told him I wasn't planning another trip to Burma and I wanted to meditate more on this trip. He responded with a glance and deafening silence. My steadfast confidence began to waiver and I suddenly had a sense that I was standing on thin ice. I further explained that I was going to be the translator for the whole event and that I was a key person for the seminar. More silence from U Pandita and an uncomfortable feeling that I was sliding further out onto the thin ice.

I continued to somewhat desperately explain that the aikido seminar was planned months ago and that I had already committed to going. Then U Pandita asked me again "What is aikido?" (This wasn't the aikido conversation I had envisioned). Somehow it was translated as a 'martial art' and there was something profoundly unsettling about the way U Pandita was looking at me. He was quite generously giving me all the rope I wanted. I was methodically wrapping it around my neck. The intensity of U Pandita's silence was like a mirror that's reflection was undeniable and I was just beginning to see it. I was choosing to leave a 2,500 year-old practice of spiritual liberation to go practice a 'martial art.' The ice began to crack.

Then, turning on me with full presence, U Pandita looked me in the eye and in English said,

"When you have spiritual protection, you don't need martial protection."

It is hard to describe the effect these words had on me in that moment. Up until then, I had invested many years in the belief that aikido was a 'spiritual' martial art. O Sensei was proof of this. I loved the martial training and had dedicated my life to its perfection. I assumed that it

204

would naturally lead me to the spiritual if I 'just kept training'. An unquestioned promise of a future enlightenment, if I just kept doing my technical aikido training. I was attached to the martial and I wasn't willing to let it go to move into the spiritual aspect that was in fact, my heart's deepest desire. Indeed, this was why I had come to Burma. I wanted to have my cake and eat it too. I was clinging to years of investment in aikido as I understood it at that time, and it was the very thing that was holding me back.

My future and past were all hanging in the balance in that very moment with an unbearable intensity. Then with those words, the ice suddenly gave way and I fell into the abyss. My knees buckled and the ground became unstable. In a moment, with one perfectly placed Zen whack, I was stripped of my identity. I was totally disoriented and was left with nothing to hold on to. My self-deception was exposed for the sham that it was, and what was revealed was what had always been there at the bottom of it all, my total insecurity. I was at a complete loss as to what to do, so I grasped for the only thing that was left. I gave in and surrendered. In that moment, I told U Pandita I wouldn't go to the seminar. With tears in my eyes I begged him to let me stay and practice. He then did something I never even conceived as being possible. He unceremoniously told me "No" and sent me away like a schoolboy.

I couldn't believe this was happening. I had been dismissed. I was thrown out. I hefted my backpack, (which was suddenly very heavy) and stumbled out of the monastery in a daze. I found my way to a taxi and about half an hour later, I was sitting in a Japanese restaurant in downtown Rangoon drinking a beer with my Japanese friend. It was totally surreal, and utterly meaningless. I was completely disoriented, and still in a daze from this ego destroying encounter with U Pandita. I did my best to engage my Japanese friend in aikido talk, as he told me how great the coming seven-day aikido seminar was going to be. Of course it wasn't.

When the time came to leave Burma, I stopped by the monastery on the way to the airport to ask U Pandita if I could return to practice on my next visit to Burma. U Pandita gave his permission and six months later, I was sitting my first three month retreat with him. My 'year of travel' turned into eight, and I spent each winter returning to Burma for meditation retreats.

A Way to Reconcile the World

You may be wondering why I am sharing this story as one of my significant, if not my most significant aikido experience. This was the point that all of the false ideas that I had built about aikido were unpleasantly exposed. I was sure of aikido's spiritual depth but I was looking for it in the wrong place. The spiritual is not to be found in the physical, nor does it exist in the martial. It can be expressed in these realms but its source is beyond. My attachment to aikido prevented me from realizing this. And this encounter with U Pandita was the beginning of correcting that mistaken view.

It was a hard lesson, but it changed my path in aikido. Indeed it changed the direction of my whole life. Because it was only when I managed to let go of what I had made important in aikido, that aikido's deeper value began to emerge.

And it happened with the words of a simple monk:

"When you have spiritual protection, you don't need martial protection".

気　気　気

Aikido and the Art of Going with the Flow
by
Molly Hale, - Aikido West - U.S.A. - 4th Dan

In the beginning

I began my study of aikido in 1984, coming to the mat through a variety of experiences. My first encounter with martial arts of any form was through one of my brothers, who practiced judo at San Jose State University under Yoshihiro Uchida. I was fascinated. My next encounter was through my then seven year-old son, Sebastian, whose school (very progressively) offered aikido. I would ferry him to and from the *dojo*, observing what he was doing in the few minutes before he bowed out. I was also intrigued by the television show with David Carradine in his role as a warrior monk, Kwai Chang Caine, in the 1970s series 'Kung Fu.'

The defining moment that brought me to consider aikido for myself came during a 10-day retreat at the Lomi School, an integrative, somatic mind-body school co-founded by Richard Strozzi-Heckler. During this retreat, we spent an afternoon at Aikido of Tamalpais, training with Robert Sanoff. I took to the training like a duck to water. At the end of the class, Robert had each one of us stand in front of him, while he executed a *shomenuchi* strike with a *bokken*. Our job? To get off the line, out of the path of harm. When it was my turn, I found myself frozen, no ducking, no covering my head, no movement. I was stunned and curious about my response. As soon as I returned home, I signed up at Aikido West under Frank Doran *Sensei*.

I trained twice a week in the basics class for 10 weeks, but then the demands of single parenthood rose up. I had to help out with Halloween costumes and parties. Then there was Thanksgiving and soon, I let my training fall away. However, one evening, I was having a particularly challenging phone conversation with my mother. I felt calm, attentive to what she was saying even though I didn't like what I was hearing. I looked down at my feet and noticed I was standing in *hanmi*. This was life-altering. Prior to my brief training in aikido, I would have interrupted, deflected, felt diminished by her words, but I stood my ground in respect, hearing the full-blown attack and was able to respond with presence and kindness.

The change in me, in my stance, sent me back to the *dojo* with a clear commitment to stay the-course.

Eleven years later

In 1995, returning home from my 11th consecutive year of aikido summer retreat in San Rafael, an absolutely stellar time. I fell asleep while driving. In an instant, that momentary lapse of awareness altered forever what I had thought was the path of my life. My vehicle rolled end over end, three and a half times, taking me and my three passengers on a beautiful forward roll. It left them physically uninjured and fortunately no other vehicle on the road was involved. Only they can speak of the impact to their emotional bodies, but I became quadriplegic in that moment with a prognosis of no volitional movement below my shoulders for the duration of my life. Whew!

Oftentimes in martial practices, the effectiveness of the art 'in the real world' comes into question. My passion and participation in aikido was based on my desire to practice peace, to polish my awareness of self and other, bringing a calmer, more perceptive, awake, tuned-in presence to the life I was living. I had originally taken a self-defense course to learn 'street smarts,' but found that aikido encompassed my connection to life's partnerships, a yielding without resistance to what 'is'. Due to its physical nature, these ideas were held in my bones, in my tissues, as well as my thinking.

It was this that I drew on as I lay in an intensive care unit, drugged, post-surgery, haloed and spastic. I drew on my inner awareness, honed by the hours and hours of *aiki* practice that had merged with dance, *continuum*, yoga, *Feldenkrais*, tai chi and acupuncture in order to cope. It proved to be life saving. Practicing joining, merging, stillness, balancing in the vortex of the spiral, connection, harmony, presence with self and community would all come into play over the days, weeks, months and years of my recovery.

Staying connected to my internal body was critical as I overheard hushed voices speaking of my prognosis; the fear and confusion in their voices, the deep concern. I recall my *Sensei*, Frank Doran, touching my body and saying,

"Molly, you have been giving and giving to us in the *dojo*. Now, your job is to receive."

And receive I did. The aikido community from far and wide created a safety net of loving compassion, some by their physical, hands-on presence in my daily life and some through their mindful presence at a distance. Every day for the two months, I spent in the hospital, my aikido family was present and after only two meals prepared in-house, they began signing up to bring me breakfast, lunch and dinner.

I was unable to feed myself, so each person spoon-fed me nutritious, health-giving foods with the tenderness of heart and clarity of purpose, supporting and maximizing my recovery.

Once this was done, they would begin massaging and stroking my body with the intention of reminding it of that with which it was most familiar, touch. One premise of aikido is to touch without doing harm. My spinal cord was damaged between C5 and C6 with most of the nerves above and below this area, fully intact, just separated from my brain. I trusted my body would respond and everyone participated in making it so.

The hospital staff were amazed that the stream of people just kept flowing. That is the nature of my aikido community. Their support of me was also supporting my still in-shock husband and family.

Returning home after two months, my care was potentially quite stressful as there was nothing I could do for myself, except talk and scratch my own nose. Jeramy, my husband, and Kyrie, our daughter, were in the position of care providers along with a home care nurse. My aikido community remained connected, continuing to come to our home and work with my body, relieving Jeramy and Kyrie of the potential overload of the work at hand. Dinners were prepared, clothes were washed, beds were changed, the garden was attended, entertainment was addressed and I was thriving.

Moving forward one year, I returned to the San Rafael summer camp in 1996, wanting to remain connected to the larger community. I was able at this point to sit and had begun training by sitting on the mat, cross-legged. I had recovered some trunk stability, but was amazingly spastic with a fetal response to stimulation. *Aikidoka* carried me onto the mat and we trained. People would carefully wrap my fingers around their wrists over-and-over, giving me the correct input to my nervous system. One day at camp, I received 15 hours of uninterrupted massage and gentle handling, with tag teams of friends, taking turns all day and into the night.

Prior to the injury to my spinal cord, I had been preparing for my third *dan* exam. Post injury, I continued to show up and train at the *dojo*, whenever I could and this led to an examination in 2001. Everyone in the *dojo* was supportive of my training and, having zero experience with training with a wheelchair user, we explored the various adaptations necessary for functional, effective expression of martial practice.

I could feel in my body the 'borrowing' from my training partners of what was ordered in their bodies, the electrical connectivity of touch flowing into my awareness. When I would train from a seated position on the mat, I was able to receive the wonderful stretching that occurs when being pinned to the mat. These partner engagements clearly supported my being able to maintain flexibility and extension. In my exam, I demonstrated both from a seated position on the mat and from my wheelchair. I was able to demonstrate effectively the ability of my body in adapting to techniques.

Here I am, almost 18 years later. I continue training and, on occasion, have the opportunity to teach. I teach inside the aikido community, the martial art community at large and, most recently, in the spinal cord and traumatic brain injury unit at the Veterans Administration in Palo Alto, California.

Aikidoka continue engaging me with their honest attacks, taking time to wrap my fingers around their wrists, taking time to stretch my body into its full range, taking the time to fully relate to the adaptations necessary for our partner practice.

I am grateful for the gift of life that aikido has given, both from the deep imprint that training has infused in my being, allowing me to embrace my abilities and from the community of people attracted to this 'Art of Peace.'

A Ki Moment

by

David Weinstock - Kannagara Jinja- U.S.A. - 3rd Dan

In October of 2008, I travelled to Awassa, Ethiopia, to offer aikido training to Tesfaye Tukulu, a very talented martial art instructor with a background in karate, tai kwon do and wu shu. A year earlier he had come to Cyprus for "Training Across Borders", an event organized through Aiki Extensions. This event brought Israeli and Arab martial artists from across the Middle East to train together in the peaceful art of aikido.

Tesfaye's gentle, powerful and respectful demeanor drew the attention of several of the teachers presenting there. Aikido ignited Tes. After the summit, he immediately began training in earnest and opened the first aikido *dojo* in Ethiopia.

Several teachers, myself included, went to Awassa to teach aikido to Tesfaye, who was co-directing the Awassa Youth Project (AYP), a tiny community center he had co-founded in the heart of the city. When I arrived, the center was bursting with activity. Kids of all ages migrated between a very small aikido *dojo*, an even smaller music room, an art nook and an outdoor area with mats. They used the mats for dance, acrobatics, and theatrical rehearsals for their circus show. Their travelling troupe raised awareness about aids and social justice issues as they performed around Africa.

The first night after I landed in Awassa, Tes and a few of the other organizers took us out on the town. After some tibs (a traditional goat dish), chororsaa- (spicey beans) and injera (Ethiopian flat bread) we went out to a bar to dance.

My son, Sam, was with us. Already a masterful tap dancer at 19 years of age, he had brought 20 pairs of tap shoes with him so that he could teach dance to the children at AYP. Also proficient at hip-hop, salsa, and other forms of dance, Sam, a tall strapping redhead, was used to having all eyes on him when he got on the dance floor. This night, as Tesfaye stepped out, all we could do was stand and stare at this young man who danced so joyfully, powerfully, gracefully and fully in his body.

Into the night we danced, tasting some of the local drink and having a lot of fun. Then at one point, out of the corner of my eye, I noticed Tes quietly escort two of the women that had come with us out of the bar. In close pursuit was a very large, muscular man. Something didn't feel right to me, so I followed them at a discrete distance. Tes ushered the two women into a taxi and as he turned around, this very large and now angry-looking man stepped up to him. I could not understand what was being said, but the tone and posturing of the big man was clearly confrontational. Later, Tes translated what had transpired.

Once outside, the man accused Tes of getting in the way of his advances toward one of the women. Clearly trying to provoke a fight, his voice grew louder as he took off his shirt and exposed his rippling muscled chest and six-pack. Looking on at this spectacle, my heart began to race. I had studied martial arts for 30 years and reflexively began to ready myself in case I was needed. In the face of this menacing posturing, Tes, surprisingly calm, looked at him and said in a clear and genuinely curious manner,

"Wow! You are really built. Where do you work out?"

The angry look on the man's face shifted to one of surprise. Somewhat dumbfounded, the man just said, "What?"

Tes said, "I was wondering where you work out? You're in incredible shape and I am looking for a new gym to work out in too."

At that point, the man's demeanor began to soften as he responded to Tes's genuine interest in something he clearly valued himself. The subject soon changed to workout regimes and it was right about that point, I went back into the bar.

Tes walked back in to the bar and did not know that I had witnessed the interaction. When I asked him what was going on, he said amicably,

"Oh nothing, I was just talking to a new friend."

My aikido teacher, Sensei Koichi Barrish, once said to me:

"When someone attacks, you surround them in kindness, a '*ki*' field" and he/she will have nothing to resist."

In that moment of impending conflict, Tes's practice kicked in. He allowed his embodied learning to lead. Creatively listening with all his senses, he waited for a moment of clarity to guide his intention into action. The above story reflects his ongoing commitment to a way of peace and the recognition that we are all in this together.

気　気　気

Up to My Boots in It
by
Przemek Gawronski - Aikido Dojo Tanren - Poland - 4th Dan

My story took place in the summer when I was aged about 17 or 18 years old. I had been practicing aikido for two to three years, and felt pretty good about it. I did, however, maintain a liking for military clothing and equipment, which will become relevant as this tale unfolds. In Poland, these were interesting times. The Communist regime had ended, but the free market was in its infancy and so the choice of goods in the shops was limited.

It happened in the town of Sztutowo, where I was visiting my girlfriend who was staying on holiday. It is a nice little tourist town, where it is possible to take a pleasant walk of about a mile through the forest to the sea. I was strolling back from the beach one Sunday afternoon, along with my dog, Gawron. He was very friendly and didn't seem to like trouble, even if that meant deserting me in my hour of need.

Suddenly four guys and a girl appeared out of nowhere. They were probably three to five years older than me. They were dressed in black leather jackets, sporting punk hair. They looked like they had not seen a shower or bath for at least a week.

Gawron wandered off as they spotted my black US Marine Corp boots and told me to take them off. The situation looked very bad, but because the boots were the only footwear I had with me, they had been really difficult to find and had cost a lot. I wasn't keen to just hand them over.

I took in the situation and considered my options from a martial perspective. Meanwhile, one of them began to shout at me to take the boots off. His language was threatening and abusive.

I played for time, hoping that maybe someone else would show up, who might be able to help me, but there was no sign of anyone. A couple of minutes passed and the punks became more and more impatient. One of them moved forward wielding a huge butcher's knife, which had previously been hidden under his jacket. He pointed it at me and said,

"We don't have all day!"

This persuaded me that this wasn't the time to try out my aikido technique. The idea suddenly seemed ridiculous. It seemed that my options were non-existent, but then I realised that that they had probably run away from home. So whilst my boots were an obvious target, the likelihood was that they were hungry and so what they really wanted was some food.

I was about to take the train back home anyway and I didn't mind giving them the food that I had left over from my stay, back at my campsite, which I would otherwise have had to pack in my backpack (a military one of course) and transport back.

With this in mind, I told them that taking my boots was a waste of time. I pointed out that it was the middle of summer and it would be very difficult to sell them, which is what I figured they had in mind. I went on to say that if they were happy to come back to my tent, I would be happy to give them a couple of spare cans of sardines, some bread and some packets of instant soup.

They looked at each other for a few moments and asked if I was joking. I told them I was not and I started walking in the direction of the campsite. The gang quickly caught me up and started walking alongside me. After a short while, I stopped and said that actually I wasn't sure that this was a fair deal. They looked at me as if I was mad.

I went on to say that I should get something from them in return. I told them that I would give them 50 zloty (about 10 pounds or fifteen dollars) if they would give me the knife that they had used to threaten me, which would allow them to buy a bottle of vodka or some beer. They seemed shocked by this proposal, and so was I, but 30 seconds later, they agreed.

Gawron came back to join us and we walked on all together for another five minutes and once at the tent, we carried out our exchange.

As they said their goodbyes, the biggest one said that if anybody gave me a hard time, I could find them camping off site, about half way to the sea and 300 meters from the street, on the right-hand side.

I now run courses on negotiation and conflict management and tell this story at every workshop, stressing that if we take the time to find out what the other party really wants, we have a much better chance of finding a solution that satisfies the needs of everyone, and as I do so, I present my souvenir, the large butcher's knife.

气 气 气

Parkinson's - The Ultimate Uke
by
Paul Linden - Aikido of Columbus - U.S.A. - 6th Dan

I have been practicing aikido for 42 years and Parkinson's disease for 10 years. Aikido is a nonviolent Japanese martial art and a study of peacemaking. Parkinson's is a degenerative disease of the brain. The two have a lot in common.

Many years ago, while visiting Los Angeles, I met a friend of a friend. As we were sitting together eating lunch, he casually said,

"You know, I could kill you as you sit there."

I smiled and said, "Yes, of course you could" and kept eating.

I knew he wasn't being hostile, but was merely expressing a fact. Astonished that I understood, he explained that he was a Vietnam veteran, and that was his way of testing me.

He had killed many people, and he knew how thin the line is between life and death. He knew that anyone could die at any moment. Combat soldiers learned to live on the edge of life and death, and when they came home, they were unable to fit back into normal society, which pretends that death won't happen. He was stunned that a non-veteran knew that edge. I told him about my martial arts training and how it was possible to know the edge without killing anyone.

Two concepts underlie aikido as I practice and teach it: First, emotions and attitudes are physiological events in the body, and to receive an attacker in a peaceful way, the body must be trained to do so. And second, the body moves with better balance and strength in a state of inner stillness, kindness, and gratitude. (My website has a free downloadable book, *Reach Out*, which details the basic exercises that I use to teach this. www.being-in-movement.com).

Practicing calmness when attacked and compassion for the attacker carries over to stresses and problems that aren't attacks, such as Parkinson's, for instance. When I was diagnosed, my initial reaction was shock. And my practice for the next six months was to say to myself many times a day "Parkinson's" and train my body to go into calmness instead of fear. Gradually stillness and compassion took the unease out of the disease.

The real function of martial arts, I think, is to help us accept our fundamental weakness. I can block a punch, I can parry a kick, and I can escape an arm lock. But I can't control the weather, a presidential election, or whether I have Parkinson's. Once we build up enough personal power, we can accept somewhat calmly the unacceptable.

Having Parkinson's is inconvenient, but if I get frustrated or irritated at it, the tremors increase and the disease feels worse. The more I meet Parkinson's with an attitude of compassionate engagement and relaxed strength, the better my body functions. This is not philosophy. It's physiology.

In addition, mindful physical exercise is an element in aikido, and it has played a major factor in slowing down the progress of the disease. I recently had physical therapy to learn some Parkinson's-specific exercise forms. The physical therapist was astounded that after 10 years I can still move well and teach aikido. It's rather elegant actually: doing aikido keeps me moving well enough to do aikido.

The questions are: What do I choose to become as Parkinson's eats away at my brain? Do I cultivate habits of fear or anger about my condition or habits of power and compassion? So in the end, practicing Parkinson's is very similar to practicing aikido.

Parkinson's will never be popular as a path of self-improvement. The same approach, though, can be applied to everyday difficulties, whether personal, interpersonal, or international. The world would be very different if people didn't respond to difficulties in a rush of fear and anger. Think of all the killing and aggression that would not take place if we each took responsibility for our own body and our hurtful reflexes. Peace would be possible.

Copyright © 2013 Columbus Dispatch

気　気　気

Glossary

agatsu	Self-victory; victory over oneself.
ai	Harmony, joining, or unification; the first part of the name 'aikido.'
aidori	A cross-hand single-wrist grab, used in aikido training.
aihanmi	A stance wherein persons facing one another place the same foot and arm forward.
aiki	The blending of energy (*ki*) or harmonizing of spirit.
aikidoka	A practitioner of aikido.
atemi	A defensive strike or movement in aikido practice, intended to distract or unbalance one's partner, or to draw attention to a martial opening or unprotected vital point.
bokken	A wooden sword used in martial arts practice.
budo	The 'martial way': cultivation of warrior discipline and the arts of protection as a life path.
buto	Dance; dancing.
chado	The 'way of tea'; the Japanese practice of tea ceremony.
chimpira	Low-level criminals or hoodlums.
continuum	The co-joining of breath, sound and movement that happens to be therapeutic.
dan	Step, grade, or degree of black belt rank in Japanese martial arts.
do	Path or way, as in 'way of life'. (Equivalent Chinese term is 'Tao' (Dao)).
dori	Grab.
Feldenkrais	A method of somatic education founded by Moshe Feldenkrais.
gi	A martial arts training uniform, usually including white trousers, wrap-around jacket, and belt. Also called *dogi*.
gyakuhanmi	A stance wherein persons facing one another place the opposite foot forward.
hajime	'Begin!'; a verbal command given by a martial arts instructor.
hakama	A traditional Japanese garment covering the lower body, resembling a long, divided, pleated skirt. Worn by many aikido practitioners, especially those with black belts.
hanbo	A short wooden staff used in martial arts practice.

hanmi	A basic triangular stance in aikido practice, standing with one foot forward. Literally: 'half body'.
hara	Literally: 'belly' or lower abdomen; a term used in aikido and other arts to refer to the 'center' from which movement and *ki* arise.
hijidori	Elbow grab.
ikebana	The traditional Japanese art of flower arranging.
ikkyo	'First teaching': a fundamental aikido technique to unbalance and pin one's partner.
irimi	'Entering': a basic principle used in aikido techniques.
iriminage	Aikido throws that utilize the principle of 'entering'.
Jainism	An Indian religion that prescribes a practice of nonviolence toward all living beings.
jo	A wooden staff used in martial arts training.
kangeiko	A formal period of intensive training that takes place during the coldest month of the year; a tradition in Japanese martial arts and other disciplines.
kado	The traditional way of flower arranging.
karateka	Practioner of karate
kata	Form; a set form in martial arts practice.
katatedori	Same-side, one-handed wrist grab.
katsuhayabi	Literally: 'victory-swift-day'; a frequent reference by the founder of aikido, thought to refer to a transcendent quality of speed, resulting from the unification of mind, body, and spirit.
ki	Universal energy or life force. Equivalent Chinese term is 'chi'.
ki breathing	A form of breathing that helps the practitioner to become calm and relaxed.
kiai	A focused shout practiced in martial arts, arising from the *hara*, which expresses confidence and power, and is thought to extend *ki* (vital energy).
kimono	A long, wide-sleeved Japanese robe worn with an *obi* (sash).
kokyu	Breath, breathing; a central concept in aikido practice. *Kokyu* refers to more than the physical breath and is associated with the extension and movement of *ki*.
kokyunage	Literally 'breath throw'; aikido techniques relying upon timing, momentum, *ki*, and 'breath'.

kotegaeshi	An aikido technique utilizing a supinating wrist lock.
kubishime	Neck choke.
kuzushi	The practice of destabilizing the balance of a partner or opponent.
kyu	Grades of promotion in aikido and other martial arts progressing toward the black belt, represented by white or coloured belts in some *dojos*.
ma-ai	Optimum distance between combatants, technically a dynamic concept incorporating velocity and vectors of attack as well as the spirit of the interaction.
masakatsu	'True (correct) victory'; often paired with the concept of *agatsu* or 'victory over oneself'.
misogi	Purification, cleansing, refinement of mind, body, and spirit; can refer to specific ascetic rituals such as prayerful physical activity while standing under a sacred waterfall.
morotedori	Both hands grab one wrist of the partner or opponent.
musubi	Connection, 'tying together', the blending or joining of mental and physical energies between partners or opponents.
nage	Throw; also the person who applies a technique.
nidan	Second-degree black belt.
nikyo	'Second teaching': a fundamental aikido technique utilizing a joint lock.
obi	The long sash tied about the waist over a Japanese kimono or martial arts uniform.
Pilates	An exercise system promoting core strength and flexibility, developed by Joseph Pilates.
randori	The freestyle practice of aikido with more than one attacker.
Rolfing	An holistic system of soft tissue manipulation and movement education that organizes the whole body in gravity, developed by Ida Rolf, often referred to as Structural Integration.
ronin	A samurai who had no feudal master in old Japan.
ryotedori	A two-hand grab, to connect with both wrists of the partner or opponent.
sandan	Third-degree black belt.
sankyo	'Third teaching': a fundamental aikido technique utilizing a wrist twist.

sensei	Teacher. A term of respect.
seiza	A traditional Japanese kneeling posture.
shihan	In aikido, an honorific term for a senior teacher.
shinkokyu	Deep breathing; also refers to breathing practices done with a spiritual focus.
shodan	The rank of first degree black belt, or a practitioner with a first-degree black belt, competent in the basic principles and practices, and ready to commence the deeper training.
shomenuchi	A straight strike to the top of the head.
shodo	The traditional Japanese art of calligraphy.
tai chi	A Chinese internal martial art and system of contemplative movement for the cultivation of health and longevity.
tanto	A wooden knife used in martial arts training.
tenkan	'Turning': a basic principle used in aikido techniques.
theravada	An ancient form of Bhuddhism.
tori	In martial arts, the person who completes a technique.
uchi-deshi	A dojo apprentice, or live-in student, who assists and studies intensively under the tutelage of a sensei.
uke	In aikido practice, the person who provides an attack, receives a technique, and takes a fall.
ukemi	The practice of receiving a technique, including proper ways to fall safely without injury to either party.
waza	Technique.
yame	'Stop!': A verbal command given by a martial arts instructor.
yang	In Taoist philosophy, the active, dynamic, creative, and masculine principle, often associated with the sun and light.
yin	In Taoist philosophy, the receptive, yielding, nurturing, and feminine principle, often associated with darkness and the earth element.
yokomenuchi	A diagonal strike to the side of the head or neck.
yonkyo	'Fourth teaching': a fundamental aikido technique utilizing pressure applied to the lower forearm.
yudansha	Those who have earned the rank of first degree black belt or above, as contrasted with *mudansha*, those with ranks below black belt.
zazen	Seated meditation in the practice of Zen Buddhism.

zendo   Meditation hall (or room) in Zen Buddhism, where seated meditation is practiced.

zori   Japanese flip-flop sandals, originally made of rice straw.

気　気　気